JEWISH COMMUNITY ORGANIZATION IN THE UNITED STATES

An Outline of Types of Organizations, Activities, and Problems

By

MAURICE J. KARPF, Ph.D.

President of the Faculty and Director,
The Graduate School for Jewish Social
Work, New York City

NEW YORK

BLOCH PUBLISHING COMPANY
"The Jewish Book Concern"

1938

Printed in
The United States of America
Press of the Jewish Publication Society
Philadelphia, Penna.

To

THE MEMORY OF

FELIX M. WARBURG

Distinguished citizen; patron of the arts and education;
outstanding philanthropist; foremost Jewish leader;
in profound appreciation of a cherished association.

CONTENTS

B. Types of Knowledge Needed

Studies in Jewish social life and practice—Studies in
Jewish social change—Studies in Jewish social Backgrounds—Research for applications.

C. Knowledge and Leadership

Leadership based on wealth, position and influence
but not on knowledge—Professional groups in Jewish
Community comparatively rarely utilized for leadership—Complex problems of Jewish life require special
equipment—Though professionally trained communal
workers becoming more readily available through
better training facilities need for career men not yet
sufficiently appreciated—Future points in that direction.

LIST OF TABLES

PREFACE

This study was prepared for the second International Conference on Jewish Social Work held in London, July 8–10, 1936. It follows closely an outline prepared by the writer, as President of the Conference, which was sent to the participating countries. The material was gathered and the manuscript prepared in 1935 and 1936 for presentation to the Conference. It has since been enlarged, revised and brought up to date.

It was the writer's aim to produce a comprehensive, though brief, outline of organized Jewish life in the United States. Since the study was primarily intended for foreign readers explanatory notes were included which some American readers may think unnecessary. They have been retained because several people who read the original manuscript insisted that many readers in the United States will find them helpful and valuable.

The writer aimed to be as factual and objective as possible. Accordingly, every effort was made at verification and documentation. Illustrative and corroborative material was used wherever possible, not excluding Chapter XI which deals with current trends and tendencies and must, necessarily, reflect the writer's point of view. In addition to serving the usual purposes, the notes and references contain additional sources for further reading and study.

A great deal of the material to be found in the following pages is published here for the first time. It is based on research over many years, which the writer, his colleagues on the faculty, and their students, have conducted. It is hoped that this study will stimulate further research on some of the problems which stand in great need of scientific investigation.

The nature of the material and the desire for brevity precluded mentioning the names of even those who have played leading roles in the different activities outlined. The problem of selection and exclusion was formidable, hence no names were included. This, however, should not be taken to indicate a lack of appreciation on the part of the writer, of the time, thought, energy, and effort spent by numberless socially-minded lay and professional people on the problems facing Jewish life in the United States, toward which they devoted themselves so wholeheartedly and to the solution of which they made such substantial contributions.

The current volume of the *American Jewish Year Book* contains much of the material in this study. The important additions consist of a topical Table of Contents which should aid the reader in obtaining an organized and comprehensive view of the entire subject; a List of Tables; a Summary; an Index of Authors and Publications; and a Subject Index. All of these should prove useful for easy reference.

Appropriate changes were made in the body of the text. Chapters II and IV were enlarged. The latter was enriched with additional immigration data and a discussion of problems and theories of Jewish adjustment. Chapter XII was added.

The writer desires to acknowledge with gratitude and appreciation the help of Mr. Harry Schneiderman, Editor of the *American Jewish Year Book*, who read the manuscript and made numerous helpful and valuable suggestions. Mr. Abraham G. Duker, Research Librarian of the Graduate School for Jewish Social Work, also was very helpful in many ways and especially in the preparation of the Bibliography and Index. Miss Mollie Weintraub and Miss Rose Levy have rendered valuable assistance in preparing the manuscript and reading proof. Grateful acknowledgment is hereby made to them and many others whose work aided the writer, directly and indirectly.

M. J. K.

New York, March, 1938.

CHAPTER I

THE JEWISH POPULATION IN THE UNITED STATES AND ITS DISTRIBUTION

It is estimated that there are approximately four and a half million Jews in the United States. They constitute a little over 3½% of the total population. Curious as it may seem there is no exact information about the number of Jews, their age and sex distribution, and to what extent they are of native or immigrant stock. This lack of information is due to the fact that the United States Census, taken every ten years, includes no questions regarding religious affiliation. Nor does it take cognizance of racial groups except to differentiate between the white and colored races. Nor are the results of the enumeration by mother-tongue, included in the decennial Federal census since 1920, a clue to the Jewish population, since comparatively few Jews claim Yiddish or Hebrew as their mother-tongue, and there is no way of differentiating between Jews and non-Jews who claim German, Russian, Polish, Roumanian and the other languages representing the countries from which comparatively large numbers of Jews came to the United States.[1]

However, those interested in Jewish life have need for accurate figures regarding the Jewish population. Attempts have therefore been made from time to time to secure the information upon which to base as reliable an estimate as possible. The most important of these consists of a study made in 1927, in connection with the decennial Census of Religious Bodies, under the auspices of the American Jewish

[1] For references and notes see pages 185–202.

Committee, in cooperation with the United States Bureau of the Census. This study, based on about 4000 inquiries sent to representative Jews in every city, town, and village that could be reached, indicated that there are about 4,230,-000 Jews in the United States.[2]

Various other studies have been made in a number of cities to determine their Jewish population. In such studies, the method usually consisted of taking the absences in the public schools on the High Holy Days, Rosh Hashanah and Yom Kippur, comparing them with absences on other days and estimating the Jewish population on that basis. This method, based on the assumption that all children, Jewish and non-Jewish, attend the public schools, is somewhat crude, for it is well known that a number of Jewish children attend school on the High Holy Days and therefore are lost in the count, and that non-Jewish children frequently take advantage of these holidays. The student of population figures will recognize a more fundamental difficulty in this method because it depends upon accurate knowledge of the size of families and age distribution. Since no accurate information with respect to the Jewish group is available on these items, the estimate must, of course, suffer.

Another method is based on Jewish mortality. The assumption here is that Jews, regardless of their affiliations in life, arrange for Jewish burials. This method too has obvious limitations, and is open to the same objections as the others. A number of refinements of these and other methods have been suggested and tried but none is entirely satisfactory. It is becoming increasingly clear that until an actual census of Jews is taken, there will be no accurate information as to the number of Jews in the United States.[3] For all practical purposes, however, the estimate given above may be assumed to be correct.

On the basis of all of these estimates it is fairly well known that the Jewish population in the United States is mainly concentrated in the large cities. The 1927 study referred to above, indicates that there are about 10,000 cities, towns, villages, and rural areas containing Jewish residents. Jews live in every city of 25,000 or over; in about 90% of the cities of 25,000 or less; in about 30% of the villages of 2,500 or less; and in about 7% of the rural areas.

This study also disclosed the facts that approximately 11% of the total population in cities having populations of 100,000 or over, are Jews; about 3% of cities between 25,000 and 100,000; about 1.6% in cities of 25,000 to 10,000; about .84% in cities of 10,000 to 5,000; about .7% in cities of 5,000 to 2,500; about .5% in rural incorporated villages; and about .15% in unincorporated rural territories. Stated differently, this study might be said to show that out of every 100 cities nearly 90 have Jewish residents; out of every 100 villages only 30 have Jewish residents; whereas in the country districts only 7 in every 100 have Jewish residents.

The foregoing figures do not give an adequate picture of the concentration of the Jewish population in the United States. This concentration may be better appreciated if it is borne in mind that 11 American cities contain 2,911,000 Jews, or approximately 69% of the total Jewish population; also, that 68 cities of 100,000 or over, have 3,553,000, or approximately 84%; that 209 cities of 25,000 to 100,000 have approximately 379,000 Jews or 9% of the Jewish population; that 461 cities between 10,000 and 25,000 have 111,700 Jews, or 2½%; that 721 cities of 5,000 to 10,000 have about 42,000 Jews or 1%; that 1321 cities of 2,500 to 5,000 have about 32,400 Jews or .8%; that 12,908 rural areas of 2,500 or less have 43,500 Jews or 1.2%; and that the rural unincorporated areas have about 66,000 Jews or 1.5% of the Jewish population in the United States.

The table below, (Table 1), based on the 1927 study, compares the Jewish with total population in these different areas. The discrepancies are striking and significant. It makes clear that the Jewish population in this country is largely an urban population. It is to be expected, therefore, that it will be subject to all the problems arising in urban communities. Some of these will be traced and discussed in the following pages.

TABLE 1

DENSITY OF JEWS IN CITIES AND RURAL AREAS
COMPARED WITH THE GENERAL POPULATION

Class of Place	Total Population		Total Jewish Population		Per Cent of Total Jewish Population
	Number	Per Cent of Total	Number	Per Cent of Total Population	
Cities 100,000 or over........	31,988,375	28.5	3,553,600	11.11	84.0
Cities 100,000—25,000.......	12,191,173	11.0	378,862	3.11	9.0
Cities 25,000—10,000........	6,942,742	6.0	111,742	1.61	2.5
Cities 10,000—5,000.........	4,997,794	4.5	41,855	0.84	1.0
Cities 5,000—2,500..........	4,593,953	4.0	32,370	0.71	0.8
Rural Incorporated Areas of 2500 or less...............	8,969,241	8.0	43,513	0.48	1.2
Rural Unincorporated Areas..	42,436,776	38.0	66,087	0.15	1.5
Total..................	112,120,054	100.0	4,222,029		100.0

From time to time efforts were made to bring about a better distribution of Jews in the United States. These were carried on by organizations which aimed at sending immigrants into the interior cities after arrangements were made for their employment there. The most important of these was The Industrial Removal Office, (I.R.O.) which functioned between 1901 and 1922. It was responsible for distributing about 79,000 people between the years of 1901 and 1917, the last year for which figures are available. The Galveston Movement was an attempt to divert part of the stream of Jewish immigrants from the Eastern port cities to the West by routing them to Galveston, Texas. This effort was organized in 1906 and was suspended in 1908 because of the depression at that time. It was resumed in 1910 but was definitely abandoned in 1914 because of the World War. A similar effort is now being made to distribute German Jewish immigrants in the interior, through the National Coordinating Committee for German Refugees. (See p. 121).[4]

Students of Jewish population usually assume that the Jewish population is somewhat older than is the general population. This is due to the fact that the Jewish population has a large proportion of immigrants who have arrived since 1880. (See p. 89.) The differentials are unknown.

A city-wide study of the youth in New York City made by the Research Department of the Welfare Council of New York City,[5] on the basis of visits to each hundredth residential address, a device which yielded interviews with 9,041 young men and women between the ages of 16 and

24, shows some very interesting results regarding the nativity of parents. Table 2, which is based on Table 1 of that study, is self-explanatory. Attention should be called to the comparatively small percentage of Jewish youth with both parents native (8.7%). It is also interesting to note that 82.1% of the Jewish parents came either from Russia, Poland, or Austria. But it should be borne in mind that New York City is not necessarily representative of the rest of the country.

TABLE 2

NATIVITY OF PARENTS OF NEW YORK CITY YOUTH
(Based on a study of every hundredth family)

Nativity of Parents	Total	Catholic (Roman)	Jewish	Protestant
NUMBER OF YOUNG PEOPLE IN STUDY...........................	9,041	4,392	2,835	1,606[a]
White........................	96.0[b]	98.9[b]	100.0	80.9[b]
Both Parents Native.........	24.3	28.3	8.7	42.5
One or both parents born in a foreign country.............	71.7	70.6	91.3	38.4
Italy.......................	21.9	44.5	0.1	1.7
Russia.....................	18.4	—	55.6	0.8
Poland.....................	6.2	5.7	10.2	0.7
Austria....................	6.5	2.2	16.3	1.0
Ireland....................	4.4	8.4	—	1.7
Germany...................	3.1	2.0	1.0	10.2
Hungary...................	1.6	1.4	2.3	1.1
England...................	1.2	0.7	0.4	4.1
Other[c], or not reported.....	8.4	5.7	5.5	17.1

[a] 208 failed to report religious affiliation.
[b] Negroes constitute the difference between this and 100 per cent.
[c] Less than 1 per cent. born in any one country.

The same study throws some light on the age distribution of Jewish youth. Table 3 compares the age and sex distribution of the 9,041 young people interviewed for this study by sex and age and compares the percentages of Jews and non-Jews. The differences between Jews and non-Jews are not very significant. In fact the discrepancies between Jewish males and females are greater than between Jews and non-Jews. However, the caution indicated in the preceding paragraph applies also here.

TABLE 3

AGE AND SEX DISTRIBUTION OF JEWISH AND
NON-JEWISH YOUTH IN NEW YORK CITY

(Based on a study of every hundredth family)

Sex and age at interview	Jewish young persons	Non-Jewish young persons[1]
TOTAL YOUNG PERSONS.............	2,835	6,206
	Percentage distribution of Total	
Under 18 years...................	24.0	24.8
18 to 20 years...................	32.6	34.5
21 to 24 years...................	43.4	40.7
Total.............	100.0	100.0
MALE...........................	1,353	2,989
	Percentage distribution of Males	
Under 18 years...................	26.2	25.2
18 to 20 years...................	33.9	33.7
21 to 24 years...................	39.9	41.1
Total.............	100.0	100.0
FEMALE........................	1,482	3,217
	Percentage distribution of Females	
Under 18 years...................	21.9	24.5
18 to 20 years...................	31.6	35.2
21 to 24 years...................	46.5	40.3
Total.............	100.0	100.0

[1] Includes 10 not reporting religious affiliation.

More or less reliable estimates have been made of the growth of the Jewish population in the United States as follows:

TABLE 4

ESTIMATES OF THE NUMBER OF JEWS IN THE U. S.
1818–1935[6]

Year of Estimate	Number of Jews
1818	3,000
1826	6,000
1840	15,000
1848	50,000
1877	229,087
1888	400,000
1897	937,800
1905	1,508,435
1907	1,776,885
1910	2,043,762
1914	2,933,874
1917	3,388,951
1920	3,604,580
1927	4,228,029
1935	4,450,000

CHAPTER II

ECONOMIC DISTRIBUTION

There is even greater paucity of information regarding the vocational distribution of Jews than regarding their vital statistics. There are no studies available on the number of Jews in commerce, industry and the professions. It is generally assumed that they are represented in commerce in much larger numbers than their proportion of the population; and that they are represented in industry mainly in the manufacture of light industries. Until comparatively recently they dominated the clothing industry, both among employers and employees. In recent years, however, the situation has been changing very perceptibly. While accurate information is not available, the clothing industry, which was at one time almost wholly Jewish, now consists of between 40% and 50% Jewish workers and a much larger percentage of Jewish owners. The Jewish workers are gradually being displaced by the Polish, Italian, Spanish, and Negro groups. This is largely because the sons and daughters of Jewish tailors do not, as a rule, enter the same field and there has been no large Jewish immigration for almost two decades to replenish the losses.[7]

A study recently published in one of the foremost American periodicals, *Fortune*, gives some interesting facts about Jewish participation in the commercial and industrial life of the United States. While the information is fairly accurate, it cannot be accepted as absolutely so. It may be summarized as follows: In domestic and international finance, American Jews play a relatively minor role. While there are a few important Jewish banks they are in no way to be compared in size or importance with the non-Jewish banks. Even the few Jewish banks have a considerable sprinkling of non-Jewish partners in them. There are very few Jewish employees in, or Jews on the boards of, non-Jewish banks. Jews are also sparsely represented in the following: on the controlling boards of brokerage houses dealing in stocks and bonds, and insurance companies; among owners and workers of heavy industry such as steel, automobiles, coal, rubber, oil, shipping and transportation; public utility boards controlling the sources of light and power. The situation is somewhat better in the light industries, such as textiles, silks, clothing, the distilling industry, tobacco industry, etc. But even in these, with the exception of clothing and textiles, where the Jews are largely represented as manufacturers and middle men, respectively, they do not play a dominant role. Jews have a large share in merchandising, a number of important department stores being owned or managed by Jews; they are relatively unimportant in the control of the daily press, magazines, advertising, radio, and other media for shaping public opinion. Not even in the amusement field, except in the cinema, do they exercise a major influence. The author insists that in the legal and medical professions, despite popular impression and anti-Semitic claims to the contrary, Jews play by no means the role usually ascribed to them, especially if legal and medical "power" is considered instead of numbers of practitioners. He concludes that "Jews do not dominate the American scene. They do not even dominate major sectors of the American scene."[8]

The foregoing refers mostly to ownership. The problem of getting information regarding participation of Jewish labor in the different fields is very much more difficult. There is no exact information regarding the number of Jewish workers in any field. A study made in 1929 of 50 trade unions located in New York City, with a total membership of 392,000, indicated that 134,000, roughly about one-third, were Jews. Two facts must be borne in mind in this connection. One is that the study was in New York City, where the Jewish population is approximately one-third of the total population, and the second is that the trade union study included the United Hebrew Trades, which are very largely Jewish. It is for this reason that the range of Jewish membership in these 50 trade unions was from about 8% in transportation and communication, to 98% in the retail salesmen's union. The fields of industry studied were: food preparation and distribution with 54% Jewish membership; needle trades, 59%; leather trades, 66%; building trades, 24%; printing trades, 17%; amusement trades, 37%; jewelry and ornament trades, 35%; and miscellaneous, 24%.[9] There can be no question that in cities where the Jewish population is less, proportionately, than in New York City these percentages would vary widely. Nor can there be any question that for the country as a whole the percentages would be much lower. Unfortunately, there are no data for comparative purposes.

A study made in 1935 throws interesting light on the distribution of Jews in various occupations. This study comprised approximately 17,000 Jews listed in the New York City directory under five typically Jewish names (Ginsberg, Friedman, Goldberg, Goldstein, Levy) and was compared with a typically non-Jewish name (Smith), listed in the same directory.[10]

Table 5 compares the distribution of Jewish and non-Jewish males in 15 occupations on the basis of this study.

TABLE 5

OCCUPATIONAL DISTRIBUTION OF JEWISH AND NON-JEWISH
MALE RESIDENTS IN NEW YORK CITY[11]

Occupation	Jews		Non-Jews	
	Number	Per cent	Number	Per cent
Total..................	13,618	100.0	4,668	100.0
1. Retail and Wholesale.......	2,364	17.4	282	6.0
2. Brokers and Sales..........	2,205	16.2	388	8.3
3. Skilled and Unskilled.......	1,875	13.8	1,047	22.4
4. Clerical and Sales..........	1,637	12.0	597	12.8
5. Needle Trade Workers......	1,455	10.7	79	1.7
6. Professional Service.........	887	6.5	295	6.3
7. Building Trade Labor.......	601	4.4	229	4.9
8. Manufacturing Est.'s........	574	4.2	85	1.8
9. Domestic and Personal......	508	3.7	629	13.5
10. Transp. & Communication...	500	3.7	431	9.3
11. Production—Managerial— General......	389	2.9	242	5.2
12. Unclassified...............	217	1.6	116	2.5
13. Semi-Professional Service....	179	1.3	49	1.1
14. City and Federal Employees.	180	1.3	188	4.0
15. Building Trades Contractor..	47	.3	11	.2

Table 6 compares the occupations of Jewish and non-Jewish females taken from the same source.

TABLE 6

OCCUPATIONAL DISTRIBUTION OF JEWISH AND NON-JEWISH FEMALE RESIDENTS IN NEW YORK CITY[12]

Occupation	Jews		Non-Jews	
	Number	Per cent	Number	Per cent
Total.............	3,487	100.0	1,365	100.0
1. Clerical and Sales..........	1,783	51.1	392	28.7
2. Professional...............	328	9.4	218	16.0
3. Needle Trade Workers......	313	9.0	68	5.0
4. Brokers and Sales..........	309	8.9	53	3.9
5. Retail and Wholesale.......	219	6.3	29	2.1
6. Skilled and Unskilled.......	213	6.1	50	3.7
7. Domestic & Personal Service.	120	3.4	467	34.2
8. Unclassified...............	59	1.7	24	1.7
9. Production—Managerial—General...................	43	1.2	16	1.2
10. Manufacturing Est.'s.......	43	1.2	1	.1
11. Semi-Professional..........	26	.8	13	1.0
12. Transp. & Communication...	19	.5	32	2.3
13. City and Federal Employees.	9	.3	2	.1
14. Building Trades............	3	.1	—	—

The foregoing two tables show some interesting variations. But it is impossible to say to what extent they are typical of the general population of New York City and of the entire country. A test was made in a comparison of the data secured from the city directory with the information available in the Federal census for the same area. The comparison is presented in Tables 7 and 8. But these data, too, while interesting and suggestive, are inconclusive, because the Jewish population is so large a factor in the census figures for this area. They do open up interesting possibilities and it is hoped that as a result of these and other studies we shall have more reliable and more revealing information on Jewish economic distribution in the United States than is now available.[13]

Table 7 compares the occupational distribution of male Jews with that of the non-Jewish population in New York

City based on the Federal census. The deviations are too obvious to require comment.

TABLE 7

Occupational Distribution of Jewish Male Residents of New York City Compared with the General Population in that City Based on the Federal Census of 1930[14]

Occupation	Jews		General Population	
	Number	Per cent	Number	Per cent
Total..............	13,319	100.0	1,087,707	100.0
1. Trade...................	4,594	34.5	230,326	21.2
2. Manufacturing and Mechanical	4,540	34.1	361,795	33.2
3. Clerical.................	1,823	13.7	112,731	10.4
4. Professional Service........	887	6.6	79,961	7.4
5. Domestic and Personal......	748	5.6	150,112	13.8
6. Transportation & Communication..................	594	4.5	124,348	11.4
7. Public Service.............	133	1.0	26,165	2.4
8. Agriculture................	—	—	1,722	.2
9. Extraction of Minerals......	—	—	431	—
10. Forestry and Fishing........			116	—

Table 8 makes the same comparisons for females.

TABLE 8

Occupational Distribution of Jewish Female Residents of New York City Compared with the General Population in that City Based on the Federal Census of 1930[15]

Occupation	Jews		General Population	
	Number	Per cent	Number	Per cent
Total..............	3,417	100.0	457,223	100.0
1. Clerical...................	1,794	52.5	110,727	24.2
2. Manufacturing and Mechanical	579	16.9	89,030	19.5
3. Trade...................	514	15.0	36,573	8.0
4. Professional Service........	354	10.4	59,518	13.1
5. Domestic and Personal......	144	4.2	146,913	32.0
6. Trans. and Communication..	23	.7	13,843	3.1
7. Public Service.............	9	.3	566	.1
8. Agriculture................	—	—	51	—
9. Extraction of Minerals......	—	—	2	—

The New York City Youth Study already referred to (See page 5, note 5) shows some interesting variations with respect to occupational distribution of Jewish and non-

Jewish youth. Table 9 is based on Table A of that study. Here it should be borne in mind, in addition to the cautions mentioned above, that this table is based on the occupations of youth and that the figures must not be expected, therefore, to correspond with those in Tables 5 to 8 inclusive. The present table is interesting mainly because of the information it gives and the comparisons it makes possible between Jewish and non-Jewish youth.

TABLE 9

OCCUPATIONAL DISTRIBUTION OF JEWISH AND
NON-JEWISH YOUTH IN NEW YORK CITY
(Based on a study of every hundredth family)

Types of Occupation	Males		Females	
	Jewish	Non-Jewish*	Jewish	Non-Jewish*
Clericals.....................	55.8	45.0	73.5	51.7
Semi-skilled.................	21.9	28.0	20.2	27.7
Proprietary and Managerial.....	8.5	3.6	1.6	0.2
Skilled.......................	6.4	9.4	0.6	0.9
Professional..................	4.2	2.8	3.4	4.7
Service.......................	1.6	5.2	0.7	14.6
Unskilled....................	1.6	6.1	—	0.2

* Figures are interpolated.

Table 10 shows some rather wide discrepancies between Jewish and non-Jewish persons of the same sex as to type of training received. It appears from this table that a larger proportion of Jewish young people than non-Jewish, have some kind of vocational training. This is especially true of Jewish females. Also, that almost twice as many Jewish females train for the commercial field (principally stenography, bookkeeping, typing, etc.) as non-Jewish females. On the other hand, almost three times as many non-Jewish females take training for the industrial fields as do Jewish females.

TABLE 10

Distribution of Jewish and Non-Jewish Young Persons in New York City, by Professional, Commercial or Vocational Training Received

(Based on a study of every hundredth family)

Kind of Business or Vocational Training Received	Jewish young persons of specified sex		Non-Jewish young persons of specified sex	
	Male	Female	Male	Female
Total employed and unemployed young persons	942	1,026	2,322	1,984
Total reporting	936	1,024	2,303	1,979
	Percentage distribution			
Without training	52.6	19.9	61.8	44.5
With training	47.4	80.1	38.2	55.5
Professional	12.5	6.3	7.8	6.2
Art or architecture	1.3	0.4	1.4	0.8
Aviation	—	—	0.2	0.1
Dancing	—	0.2	0.1	0.5
Dentistry or dental hygiene	0.1	0.3	—	0.1
Drafting	1.0	—	1.7	—
Dramatic art	0.3	0.1	—	0.2
Dress design	0.2	0.5	0.2	1.1
Engineering	2.1	—	1.9	—
Interior decorating	0.1	—	0.1	0.3
Journalism	0.4	0.1	0.2	—
Law	1.6	—	0.3	—
Library science	0.1	—	—	—
Medicine	—	—	0.1	—
Music	1.2	0.6	0.7	0.3
Nursing (trained)	—	0.2	—	0.7
Physical education	0.2	—	0.1	0.1
Teaching	2.5	3.8	0.3	1.6
Other	1.4	0.1	0.6	0.4
Commercial	26.2	71.0	17.1	40.9
Accounting	7.5	1.4	1.7	0.1
Advertising	0.5	0.1	0.1	—
Banking or finance	1.0	0.2	1.1	0.1
Salesmanship	0.2	0.1	0.3	0.1
Stenography, bookkeeping, typing, etc.	16.9	62.4	13.2	36.1
Private secretarial	0.1	6.8	0.8	4.5
Industrial	8.5	2.1	12.3	6.2
Auto mechanics	1.3	—	2.0	—
Aviation mechanics	0.7	—	0.8	—
Carpentry	0.2	—	1.4	—
Dressmaking or millinery	—	1.8	—	5.3
Electrical	1.7	—	3.7	0.1
Plumbing	0.4	—	0.3	—
Printing	1.3	—	1.1	—
Radio mechanics	0.2	—	0.3	—
Other	2.7	0.3	2.7	0.8
Personal service	0.1	0.7	0.4	1.9
Beauty culture or barbering	0.1	0.6	0.4	1.1
Other	—	0.1	—	0.8
Other	0.1	—	0.6	0.3
Total	100.0	100.0	100.0	100.0

Of similar interest are the data presented in Table 11, based on Table 5 of the same study. This table is interesting primarily because of the comparatively slight differences between the Jewish and non-Jewish groups. Larger variations might be expected on the basis of popular impressions.

TABLE 11

TRAINING PREFERENCES OF JEWISH AND
NON-JEWISH YOUTH IN NEW YORK CITY
(Based on a study of every hundredth family)

Type of Training Preferred	Males		Females	
	Jewish	Non-Jewish*	Jewish	Non-Jewish*
1. Employed Young People				
No training desired.........	67.1	66.7	70.8	72.1
Professional...............	11.5	9.9	11.9	8.9
Commercial...............	8.5	5.8	8.4	10.7
Academic.................	6.2	5.6	7.5	3.1
Industrial................	5.1	10.4	0.6	2.4
Other vocational...........	1.6	1.7	0.8	3.3
2. Unemployed Young People				
No training desired........	52.3	60.2	65.7	63.8
Professional...............	15.5	11.9	8.0	9.8
Industrial.................	12.0	15.9	1.7	3.9
Academic.................	10.9	4.1	8.3	3.4
Commercial...............	8.2	5.8	14.2	14.6
Other vocational...........	1.1	2.3	2.1	4.7

* Figures are interpolated.

The agricultural activities of the Jews in the United States date back about 50 years. Organized activity, however, began at the turn of this century. The foremost Jewish organization dealing with this aspect of Jewish economic life in the United States is the Jewish Agricultural Society, organized by the Baron de Hirsch Fund. In the thirty-six years of its functioning, it has spent about $3,800,-000 in aiding Jewish farmers. It estimates that about 1,500,000 acres are owned by Jews, and that there are approximately 16,000 families devoting their time, in whole or in part, to farming. The aggregate loans made to Jewish farmers by this organization amounted to about $7,500,000, in forty states, made possible by a loaning fund which rotates. This represents a remarkable growth for there was a time when there were very few Jewish farmers in the United States. There are, however, no large Jewish agricultural enterprises. Jewish agricultural endeavor consists mainly of small farms, some of which cater to vacationists during the summer months. There is a Jewish school for farming which has been in existence for forty years. It has not been outstandingly successful, for the majority of its graduates entered other occupations than that for which they were prepared in the School.[16]

Among the professions, Jews are most heavily represented in medicine, law and accounting. Here, too, it is commonly believed that they exceed by far their numerical proportion in the population. This has, in fact, been one of the problems with which far-sighted Jewish leaders have been concerned. There is everywhere evident a feeling that wisdom dictates a better distribution in these fields. This is due mainly to a growing tendency toward limitation of Jewish applicants in schools of medicine and law and to ever-decreasing opportunities for Jewish practitioners in these two professions. It is common practice in the United States for graduates of a medical school to have a year or more of internship in a hospital. In a large number of states, such internship is a prerequisite for a license to practice medicine. Jewish graduates find it extremely difficult, and in some parts of the country practically impossible, to secure interneships in non-Jewish hospitals. Similarly, Jewish physicians as a rule find it difficult or impossible to secure appointments to staffs in non-Jewish hospitals.[17] There has been some agitation for Jewish medical schools. Thus far the preponderant opinion has been that it would be unwise to create such institutions.[18]

The situation in the legal field does not lend itself to the same type of discrimination. But there are numerous evidences of fairly intense feeling in legal circles against the large number of Jews in the profession. Some of the better law schools in the country have an unofficial quota for Jewish students. Many legal or bar associations, which frequently influence, if they do not dominate the examinations for license to practice law in the different states, directly or indirectly discriminate against Jewish applicants. From time to time statements appear which, though unofficial in character, are nevertheless significant because of their sources, that Jews in these professions engage in unethical practices. Although it must be obvious to any fair-minded person that such unethical practices as exist are by no means limited to Jews, the charge is, nevertheless, leveled against them. Thus far, no concerted effort has been made to prove or disprove such charges or to deal with the problem from a long-range point of view.

The accounting profession is more or less similar to those already discussed, but since the accountant usually functions in relation to a business organization, which is his client, there is an automatic and fairly effective check on the opportunities for Jewish accountants.

A profession which is becoming more and more restricted for Jews is that of teaching in the primary and secondary schools and universities. Though the primary and secondary schools are financed from tax funds, there is a growing discrimination against Jewish teachers. In the larger cities, it is comparatively easy for Jews to secure positions in the public schools, and considerable numbers are employed in them. In the smaller communities, it is extremely difficult and in some instances practically impossible for Jews to secure teaching positions. This is due not only to discrimination against Jews but to the fact that the teacher is expected to participate in the religious life of the community. Since the Jewish teacher cannot easily do this in a Christian community, the situation becomes embarrassing and frequently impossible for him. This is not an exclusively Jewish problem since Catholics face similar situations in many communities. There are many instances in which Jewish young men and women fail to give their religious affiliation or will indicate affiliation with non-denominational religious groups, such as Ethical Culture, Quakers, etc., in order to secure positions. But even such methods are no longer effective, for among school boards, school superintendents, and teachers' employment agencies, it is commonly assumed that when one indicates "no religious affiliation" or "Ethical Culture" etc., the applicant is very likely Jewish.

In university teaching, the situation is much more aggravated. It is very difficult these days for Jews to become full professors in the leading universities. In order to attain such rank, they must have achieved distinction in their respective fields of national and international character. While Jews constitute a considerable proportion of the student bodies in the colleges and universities throughout the land, certainly much more than their numerical proportion, they represent but an insignificant proportion of the faculties. This situation is very serious because Jews are gradually being eliminated from the educational field and will ultimately be charged with making no contribution to it.

Recently, largely due to the depression during the past seven years, economic opportunities for Jews have become progressively more restricted. Office work for Jewish stenographers, typists, bookkeepers and clerical workers is extremely difficult to obtain. There are large employers of such labor, especially the large corporations, which will not employ Jewish help. To make the situation worse, there are some Jewish firms which discriminate against Jewish applicants. In all of these fields, therefore, economic opportunities for Jews are constantly contracting.[19]

There is, of course, no official governmental restriction against Jews. They are to be found in considerable numbers among the civil service employees in city, state and national government, although it must be admitted that here, too, there is some under-cover discrimination. To the student of this problem, it is easily evident that the Jew faces difficulties in every field of endeavor. Newspaper advertisements for workers occasionally carry such statements as "gentiles only," although they are less frequent than commonly supposed. This is probably due to a policy on the part of the newspapers against them. The reasons for these attitudes are many and varied. They are frequently contradictory. Studies which have been made indicate that the reasons cover the entire gamut of undesirable characteristics which the Jewish employee is presumed to possess. Most often they are given as "aggressiveness," "over-weening ambition," "radicalism," "trade-union activity," "unreliability," "loudness," "bad manners," etc.[20]

Jewish leaders have been concerned with this problem. Thus far, however, it is only in the discussion stage. While everyone seems to be aware of it, while some have given public expression of their uneasiness and feeling that something must be done about it, nothing of a concerted nature has thus far been undertaken. It requires the type of thinking, planning, and resources which are apparently not yet available in organized Jewish life in the United States.[21] However, there is some evidence that communities are awakening to the problem and are organizing themselves to meet it. Several communities have created vocational agencies. Although these have thus far concentrated their efforts on finding employment for the unemployed they are beginning to study the problems of vocational distribution as well as vocational and educational guidance.

CHAPTER III

JEWISH, NON-JEWISH RELATIONSHIPS

Although it has been estimated that there are about fifty organizations, large and small, whose dominant motif is anti-Semitism, there is no general or nation-wide organization for purely anti-Semitic purposes. Such organizations as do exist or have existed in the past, such as the Ku Klux Klan, the Silver Shirts, etc., usually include opposition to other minority groups in their program. Thus the Ku Klux Klan opposed Catholics and Negroes as well. The Black Legion, an organization similar to the Ku Klux Klan, came into prominence in 1936. The state of Michigan was the main field for its activities which included a series of murders. Its hostile agitation was directed against all non-Protestant groups. However, from time to time, organizations and activities appear which do aim at the Jews. Such an organization was the Silver Shirts, with its various publications; the *Dearborn Independent*, financed by Henry Ford, the automobile magnate, who later retracted and apologized to the Jewish people; and a number of others. There are also other activities on the American scene which have an anti-Semitic tinge. The activities of Father Coughlin, the radio priest, and the successors to the late Senator Huey Long from Louisiana, who set up a virtual dictatorship in that state, and was aiming for the Presidency of the United States, may be included in this category.

Happily, these groups and activities have had no governmental support whatsoever. On the contrary, there is ample
evidence that the American government, and in the vast
majority of instances, the state and local governments, are
opposed to any type of anti-Semitic activities just as they
are opposed to any other activities tending to create racial
strife. But it must be recognized that the racial and religious
questions are latent if not active in the American scene.
One need only recall the Presidential campaign of 1928,
when Alfred E. Smith, former Governor of the state of New
York, the most outstanding Catholic layman and statesman
at the time, was the democratic candidate for President,
and the campaign of religious prejudice and bigotry on the
basis of the Catholic issue which was waged against him,
to appreciate what can be done. Similiarly, one need only
think of the situation of the Negroes in the South, the prejudice against them, the frequent acts of mob violence and
lynching of Negroes, the social, economic, and political discrimination practiced against them in the South, as well
as race riots in Northern cities, to realize that racial and
religious antagonisms and conflicts are neither unknown nor
impossible in the United States.

From time to time there appear pamphlets, articles, and
books, which indicate that the Jewish issue is not far from
the surface, and that it would require comparatively little
provocation to bring it to the surface. On the other hand,
a number of Jews hold prominent positions in American
public life. In 1932, the Governors of the States of Illinois,
New York, Oregon and New Mexico, were Jews. The first

two states have large Jewish populations, but the number of Jews in the last two is negligible. Two of the outstanding liberal judges on the Supreme Court of the United States, the highest court in the land, are Jews, and they are universally respected for their legal scholarship, humanitarianism, and courage. There are now, and there have been almost from the beginning of this Republic, Jews in the Congress of the United States. Other Jews prominent in the judicial, diplomatic and other public services might be mentioned as proof that there is no official anti-Semitism in the United States.[22]

The provocation for bringing the anti-Jewish question into the open, in fact almost creating the issue, was unfortunately provided in the depression which has lasted for almost seven years. In all such situations, a scapegoat is sought, and any convenient one seized upon. Several attempts have been made to use the Jew and Jewish influence in governmental affairs, especially in the Roosevelt administration, as this convenient scapegoat. The developments in Germany and the Hitler propaganda in the United States and elsewhere have seriously aggravated the situation. The enormous publicity which has been given in the American press to the Nazi attitudes, programs, and activities against the Jews, has not strengthened the Jewish position in the United States, although there are innumerable gentiles who are incensed at what Nazi Germany is doing.[23]

The national election campaign of 1936 was of tremendous importance from the standpoint of the fear and insecurity which it aroused in Jews and liberal-minded non-Jews,

because of the anti-Jewish propaganda in which the opponents of President Roosevelt engaged. His remarkable
victory left no doubt that anti-Semitism is not a safe campaign issue in the United States.

Various attempts have been made to deal with the situation. The propaganda against the Nazis and their regime;
the identification of the type of discrimination against Jews,
with discriminations either immediate or ultimate against
other minority groups; the stimulation of labor and other
liberal groups to the realization that Nazi Germany and
its program represent a threat to them; the boycott against
Germany, and especially the non-Jewish participation in
the boycott; the coupling of the present German government's activity against the Jews with its war activities and
threats to the peace of the world; all of these are aspects
of the efforts at combating not only the German influence
in this country but also the rise of anti-Semitism and intolerance in whatever guise.

It is impossible to estimate the results of these activities.
Many believe that were the Jews to present a united front
to the world in these and other efforts, however much they
might differ internally, a great deal more could have been
accomplished. Others view the situation differently and
hold that a united front could be accomplished only through
compromise and more can be achieved by each group pursu-
ing its own program vigorously.[24]

One of the safeguards in the Jewish position in the United
States rests in the relationship between the different religious
groups. While there can be no doubt that there is consid-

erable antagonism between Protestants and Catholics, and between them and the Jews, there is also no doubt that, in so far as the organized activities of these groups are concerned, there is every desire, both official and unofficial, for cooperation, understanding, and tolerance.

There are numerous inter-racial and inter-religious activities which aim at bringing about better understanding between the different groups, making up the body politic in American life. One organization in particular, The National Conference of Jews and Christians, might be mentioned in this connection. Others are doing no less important work.

Another safety factor in the situation is the fact that the United States is a country where democracy is passionately believed in, and that although it is sometimes spoken of as "a Christian country," and occasionally even as "a Protestant country," it is, nevertheless, made up of many religious elements. This diversity in population prevents the type of homogeneity necessary for breeding racial, social, and religious bigotry which fertilizes the soil for anti-Semitism. There is also an awareness on the part of at least the liberal and intelligent groups in American life that the greatness of the United States is not due to any one religious or cultural group but that all groups from all corners of the world have contributed to its development. There is an appreciation that would be difficult to find in other countries, of the contribution which each cultural group can make toward the sum total of American culture. Indeed there are those who think of American culture as a fusion of the world cultures which have gone into the so-called "melting pot" and which have created the America of today.[25] In addition to these must be mentioned the fact that there is no tradition of Jewish persecution in this country. Americans cannot forget that their country was founded and developed by those who sought to escape from religious persecution abroad.

CHAPTER IV

IMMIGRATION, EMIGRATION AND JEWISH ADJUSTMENT

A. Present Attitudes Toward Immigration

The day when the United States had a wide open door for immigrants is, it is feared, gone forever. While in a sense there has been some type of restriction of immigration for almost 100 years, real restriction did not begin until the adoption of the Quota Law in 1921.[26] Whereas originally immigrant legislation aimed at protecting the immigrant, recent legislation aimed in the beginning at selection, and later almost exclusively at restriction. This new restrictive legislation had its origin in the social and economic conditions of the country. Today, largely as a result of the problems which arose during the World War and the economic crisis since 1929, immigration into the United States is very limited. Officially and unofficially the government has been opposed to large immigration. In fact such quotas as exist have not been filled[27] and efforts are being made in the Congress, to reduce even existing limited quotas. Whether the restrictionist forces will be successful or not, there can be no denying the fact that large scale immigration into the United States is out of the question for the present and the immediate future. Despite this, government officials in the present administration have adopted a generous and liberal attitude regarding German refugees. Considerable numbers have come to the United States and are gradually adjusting themselves here. But opposition is heard from time to time and agitation has started against them. Occasionally one hears statements in the Congress of the United States to the effect that the traditional policy of this country being a refuge for those who are persecuted in other lands has been abandoned. No one who knows the situation can have much hope that the immigration policy of the United States will become less restrictive than it is now. On the contrary, the tendency is for more restriction, and it is likely that the next few years will see further restrictive legislation.

This is largely due to the attitudes of what are sometimes called "100 percenters," those who have at other times been called the "Know-Nothings" because of their distrust of and opposition to others than native Americans. But even liberal groups, such as organized labor, are opposed to immigration. This is because they view the opportunities in America as constantly diminishing. They believe, therefore, that immigrants coming to this country take the places which would otherwise go to unemployed Americans. The fact that so many millions of Americans have been unemployed for a period of years, that even now, when the depression is easing, there are still between seven and eight million people unemployed, constitutes a powerful argument against a liberal immigration policy. This the labor groups and others are not reluctant to use.

B. Immigration Statistics and Their Significance

In the 56 years, 1881 to 1936 inclusive, there came to the
United States nearly 28 million (27,829,121) immigrants,
of whom almost two and a half million (2,416,916), were

TABLE 12

TOTAL AND JEWISH IMMIGRATION TO THE UNITED STATES,
1881–1936

Year	Total	Jews	Per Cent of Total	Year	Total	Jews	Per Cent of Total
1881	669,431	5,692*	.9	1909	751,786	57,551	7.7
1882	788,992	13,202	1.7	1910	1,041,570	84,260	8.1
1883	603,322	8,731	1.4	1911	878,587	91,223	10.4
1884	518,592	11,445	2.2	1912	838,172	80,595	9.6
1885	395,346	16,862	4.3	1913	1,197,892	101,330	8.5
1886	334,203	21,173	6.3	1914	1,218,480	138,051	11.3
1887	490,109	33,044	6.7	1915	326,700	26,497	8.1
1888	546,889	28,881	5.3	1916	298,826	15,108	5.1
1889	444,427	25,352	5.7	1917	295,403	17,342	5.8
1890	455,302	28,639	6.3	1918	110,618	3,627	3.0
1891	560,319	51,398	9.2	1919	141,132	3,055	2.6
1892	579,663	76,373	13.2	1920	430,001	14,292	3.3
1893	439,730	35,322	8.0	1921	805,228	119,036	14.7
1894	285,631	29,179	10.2	1922	309,556	53,524	17.3
1895	258,536	26,191	10.1	1923	522,919	49,719	9.5
1896	343,267	32,848	9.6	1924	706,896	49,989	7.0
1897	230,832	20,372	8.8	1925	294,314	10,292	3.5
1898	229,299	23,654	10.7	1926	304,488	10,267	3.3
1899	311,715	37,415	12.0	1927	335,175	11,483	3.4
1900	448,572	60,764	13.5	1928	307,255	11,639	3.8
1901	487,918	58,098	12.1	1929	279,678	12,479	4.5
1902	648,743	57,688	8.9	1930	241,700	11,526	4.8
1903	857,046	76,203	8.9	1931	97,139	5,692	5.9
1904	812,870	106,236	11.8	1932	35,576	2,755	7.7
1905	1,026,499	129,910	12.6	1933	23,068	2,372	10.3
1906	1,100,735	153,748	13.4	1934	29,470	4,134	14.0
1907	1,285,349	149,182	11.6	1935	34,956	4,837	13.8
1908	782,870	103,387	13.2	1936	36,329	6,252	17.2
				Total	27,829,121	2,419,916	8.7

* Data from 1881 to 1898 include only ports of New York, Philadelphia and Baltimore

Jews. Table 12 gives the total and Jewish immigration
figures for this period, year by year. It shows that the ratios
of Jewish to general immigration, ranged from less than
1% in 1881, to more than 17% in 1922 and 1936. But, as
will be observed, the increase in ratio was neither continuous
nor sustained beyond the first ten years. After 1892 it rose

and fell until it reached a high point (17.3%) in 1922. This was no doubt due to the accumulation of would be immigrants during the World War years when Jewish immigration was at a low level because it was impossible to leave the East-European countries, at that time the main source of Jewish immigration. Thereafter, it dropped again, due to the restrictive legislation introduced in 1922, until 1933, when it began to rise again and reached its highest point (17.21%) in 1936.

It should be noted, however, that although the ratios of Jewish to general immigration in the years 1933 to 1936 are among the highest in the history of Jewish immigration to the United States, the absolute figures of Jewish immigrants are the lowest in the entire period except during 1918 and 1919, influenced by the War. This seeming paradox is explainable by the drop in general and Jewish immigration since 1931, owing to the depression and the consequent tightening of granting visas during President Hoover's administration. The great need of German-Jewish refugees since 1933, due to the Hitler regime, and the more generous attitude of President Roosevelt's administration toward those suffering from persecution and discrimination in Germany, doubled and trebled the number of Jewish immigrants of 1932 and 1933. However, the total number of immigrants increased but slightly due to the unattractive economic conditions in the United States. The striking similarity between the ratios of the general and Jewish immigration, by decades, since 1911, and their respective totals, (Table 13), is of special interest in this connection.

TABLE 13
Total and Jewish Immigration to the United States, 1881–1936, by Decades

Decade	Total Immigrants	Per Cent of Total	Jewish Immigrants	Per Cent of Total
1881–1890................	5,246,613	19.0	193,021	8.0
1891–1900................	3,687,564	13.2	393,516	16.2
1901–1910................	8,795,386	31.5	976,263	40.3
1911–1920................	5,735,811	20.5	491,120	20.3
1921–1930................	4,107,209	14.8	339,954	14.1
1931–1936................	256,538	1.0	26,042	1.1
Total................	27,829,121	100.0	2,419,916	100.0

TABLE 14
Total and Jewish Emigrants from the United States, 1908*–1936

Year	Departures		Per Cent to Admissions		Net Increase**	
	Total	Jews	Total	Jews	Total	Jews
1908........	395,073	7,702	50.46	7.44	387,797	95,685
1909........	225,802	6,105	30.0	10.60	525,984	51,446
1910........	202,436	5,689	19.43	6.8	839,134	78,571
1911........	295,666	6,401	33.67	7.01	582,921	84,822
1912........	333,262	7,418	39.76	9.20	504,910	73,177
1913........	308,190	6,697	25.7	6.60	889,702	94,633
1914........	303,338	6,826	24.89	4.94	915,142	131,225
1915........	204,074	1,524	62.46	5.75	122,626	24,973
1916........	129,765	199	43.42	1.31	169,061	14,909
1917........	66,277	329	22.43	1.89	229,126	17,013
1918........	94,585	687	85.51	18.9	16,033	2,940
1919........	123,522	373	87.51	12.2	17,610	2,682
1920........	288,315	358	67.05	2.5	141,686	13,934
1921........	247,718	483	30.76	4.1	557,510	118,553
1922........	198,712	830	64.2	1.5	110,844	52,694
1923........	81,450	413	15.57	.83	441,469	49,306
1924........	76,789	260	10.8	.52	630,107	49,729
1925........	92,728	291	31.51	3.0	201,586	10,001
1926........	76,992	341	25.2	3.3	227,496	9,926
1927........	73,366	224	21.8	1.9	261,809	11,259
1928........	77,457	253	25.21	2.17	229,798	11,386
1929........	69,203	189	24.74	1.51	210,475	12,290
1930........	50,661	299	20.96	2.59	191,039	11,227
1931........	61,882	319	63.70	5.60	35,257	5,373
1932........	103,295	452	290.35	16.41	−67,719	2,303
1933........	80,081	384	347.15	16.19	−57,013	1,988
1934........	39,771	319	134.96	7.72	−10,301	3,815
1935........	38,834	330	111.09	6.82	−3,878	4,507
1936........	35,817	308	98.59	4.93	512	5,944
Total.....	4,375,061	56,003	34.52	5.08	8,300,723	1,046,311

* No figures of departures available before 1908.
** Figures arrived at by deducting departures from number of immigrants for respective years given in Table 12.

This raises the interesting question whether and to what extent Jewish immigration is influenced by economic conditions in the countries of origin and in the United States. Table 14, giving the total and Jewish departures from the United States since 1908, the first year for which such figures became available, throws interesting light on this question. This table shows that whereas the total departures from the United States since 1908 amounted to nearly 4,400,000, or almost 35% of the admissions during the same period, only 56,000 Jews, or about 5% of the Jewish admissions, left this country. Even more significant is the comparison of Jewish and total departures during the years 1932 to 1936. In each of these years there were as many emigrants as immigrants, and in two years (1932 and 1933) there were three or more times as many departures as admissions. There was, therefore, an actual loss of population during these years, no doubt due to the economic depression. The figures of Jewish departures are in striking contrast. It would appear that Jews are neither deterred from coming to the United States nor are they inclined to leave this country, once here, by adverse economic conditions in this country.

It should be borne in mind, in this connection, that Jewish immigration was always influenced by political and social pressures as well as by economic needs. This is as true today of the German immigration as it was of the immigrants from Eastern-Europe during the years 1881 to 1922. It follows that Jews were not as responsive to fluctuating economic conditions as were some of the other immigrants who sought only economic improvement.

Table 15 shows that Jews have a lower percentage among those barred from admission to and deported from the United States. In the latter category they have a decidedly

TABLE 15

TOTAL AND JEWISH IMMIGRANTS BARRED AND DEPORTED AFTER ADMISSION TO THE UNITED STATES, 1899–1936

Year	Debarred				Deported			
	Number		Per Cent to Admission		Number		Per Cent of Net Increase	
	Total	Jews	Total	Jews	Total	Jews	Total	Jews
1899–1910......	116,255	10,785	1.2	1.0	12,177	1,303	—	—
1911..........	22,349	1,999	2.5	2.1	2,788	209	.5	.2
1912..........	16,057	1,064	1.9	1.3	2,456	191	.4	.2
1913..........	19,938	1,224	1.6	1.2	3,461	253	.4	.2
1914..........	33,041	2,506	2.7	1.9	4,137	317	.4	.2
1915..........	24,111	1,398	7.3	5.2	2,670	68	2.1	.2
1916..........	18,867	949	6.3	6.2	2,906	79	1.8	.5
1917..........	16,028	607	5.4	3.5	1,918	46	.9	.3
1918..........	7,297	222	6.5	6.0	796	27	4.9	.9
1919..........	8,626	199	6.1	6.5	3,102	17	17.6	.7
1920..........	11,795	268	2.7	1.8	2,762	53	1.9	.4
1921..........	13,779	1,195	1.7	1.0	4,517	134	.8	.1
1922..........	13,731	1,256	4.4	2.3	4,345	214	3.9	.4
1923..........	20,619	1,455	3.9	2.9	3,661	99	.82	.02
1924..........	30,284	1,754	4.3	3.5	4,294	113	.68	.2
1925..........	25,390	1,137	8.6	11.1	9,495	250	4.7	2.5
1926..........	20,550	871	6.7	8.4	10,904	175	4.7	1.7
1927..........	19,755	1,090	5.9	9.4	11,662	184	4.4	1.6
1928..........	18,839	898	6.1	7.7	11,625	213	5.1	1.9
1929..........	18,127	610	6.48	4.89	12,908	153	6.13	1.25
1930..........	8,233	275	3.41	2.39	16,631	164	8.71	1.46
1931..........	9,744	405	10.03	7.12	18,142	150	51.46	2.79
1932..........	7,064	314	19.86	11.40	19,426	147	—	6.38
1933..........	5,527	276	23.96	11.64	19,865	138	—	6.94
1934..........	5,384	211	18.27	5.10	8,879	114	—	2.99
1935..........	5,558	208	15.90	4.30	8,319	96	—	2.13
1936..........	3,020	157	8.31	2.51	9,195	107	—	1.80
Total 1899–1936	519,968	33,333	2.65	1.73	213,041	5,014	—	0.28

lower percentage than the general population. This again points to the conclusion that once having received the privilege of entering the United States they will not endanger their remaining here. Detailed studies of immigration and emigration prove conclusively that Jews came to the United States as permanent settlers and, as suggested above, they were relatively less influenced than were other groups by economic conditions in this country, either in their immigration or emigration.[28] In recent years there was some emigration to Palestine, but the number of American Jews going there has been small.

During the period of heavy Jewish immigration, a number of organizations came into being for the purpose of facilitating the immigrants' adjustment in this country. Chief among these are the Hebrew Immigrant Aid Society and the National Council of Jewish Women. Both organizations cooperate with similar groups in other countries, notably the HICEM, an organization with headquarters in Paris, created by the Hebrew Immigrant Aid Society (HIAS), and the Jewish Colonization Association (ICA), so as to be of maximum help to the immigrant before arriving in this country. Once he is here, he may be aided, if he needs assistance, by either of the above organizations or by the local social service organizations.

C. Problems of Immigrant Adjustment

The heavy Jewish immigration between 1881 and 1915, raised a great many problems for the Jewish communities in which the immigrants settled. Chief among these were the problems of social and economic adjustment. Difficult as was the problem of aiding the immigrants to adjust economically, it could be done after a fashion by finding jobs for them or training them for new occupations, sending them to communities where their opportunities might be better, (See page 5) and by aiding them during the transitional period.

Much more difficult was the problem of social adjustment. At first there was no real appreciation of what this involved. The older settlers were concerned only with facilitating the Americanization of the immigrant. They believed that all that was necessary to make the "foreigner" a full-fledged American was to teach him the English language, American history, the elementary principles of civil government, and to influence him to become a naturalized citizen. Accordingly they encouraged the immigrant to abandon his former modes of life and thought, and urged him to acquire American manners and dress, thinking that they were thus speeding up the process of Americanization.

This was true of the non-Jews as well. The "one hundred percent Americans" assumed that the "foreigner" had little to give up and that he should be delighted with and thankful for the opportunity to become an American. They were disappointed when the "foreigner" did not respond in the expected manner. He was not so ready as they thought he should be, to forswear old allegiances. It seemed as if there were an adherence to traditions and memories which the Americans thought quite inferior, but which to the "foreigner" were part of him and which he was reluctant to abandon.

At first this reluctance on the part of the immigrants to accept the ready made notions of Americanization was looked upon as stubborness, wilfulness, and not infrequently, ingratitude. Gradually, however, the more thoughtful Americanization workers realized that those "foreigners" who abandoned their former modes of life most readily were by no means the best of their respective groups, and that a too rapid change seemed to go hand in hand with personal and family disorganization.

Several influences were responsible for this new appreciation of the value of the immigrant's culture. A number of settlements, notably Hull House of Chicago, due to the great humanitarianism, rare insight, and sympathy of its Head Resident, Jane Addams, emphasized the need for encouraging immigrants and their children to a full appreciation of their own culture. They encouraged the immigrants to respect and take pride in their own folk-lore, folk dances, folk music, and to express themselves in the artistic and cultural forms with which they were familiar and which had emotional value for them.

Another very important influence was a series of Americanization studies undertaken and published with the help of the Carnegie Corporation of New York. This Corporation made it possible for several of the most prominent sociologists in the United States to study the problem of Americanization. A series of studies resulted which indicated the need for a modification of the Americanization methods current at the time.[28a] Americanization workers were eager for new light because they recognized the ineffectiveness of their work. Under the guidance of the findings of the sociologists they began to recognize that the immigrant was not always as poor culturally as they had formerly assumed. Also, that those seemed to be desirable Americans who had group and cultural loyalties. They realized, as never before, that it was not to the best interests of America or the immigrants, that Americans be made overnight. The concepts of Americanization and assimilation acquired a deeper meaning. They came to be looked upon as processes which require giving as well as taking on the part of the immigrants. Similarly, that the Americanization process is reciprocal and that Americans had a great deal to gain from the cultures of older peoples.[28b] Americanization programs were considerably modified. Settlements began to encourage those whom they endeavored to serve, to celebrate their own as well as the American holidays. American ideals and institutions were presented and explained to them in the light of their own ideals and institutions, with which they were most familiar. The factory method of Americanization, which called for a mechanical uniformity, gave way to the educational method. Tolerance for the ways and feelings of the immigrant gradually replaced intolerance. Mutual trust and confidence between the immigrants and Americanization workers displaced distrust, and attitudes were developed which could not but result in the immigrants' sharing the sentiments and memories of the American people, which, the sociologists insisted, is essential to real assimilation.

The change in attitude and procedure in the general field had its counterpart in the Jewish field. The Jewish and non-Jewish settlements working in Jewish neighborhoods became more appreciative of the adherence on the part of the Jewish immigrants to their social and religious customs and practices. The resentment which the immigrants felt toward the older Jewish settlers who came from "uptown" to Americanize them and who looked down upon the "foreigners," "greenhorns," and "immigrants," was eased, and a better understanding developed than would have been possible if the older procedure for Americanizing immigrants had continued to hold sway.

It took several decades for this better understanding to develop. During the interim, the newer arrivals, dissatisfied as they were with what was being done for them, and more especially with the manner in which it was being done, frequently created their own agencies for meeting the needs of the newcomers. As the immigrant communities became larger and as the first problems of making a living were solved, they also developed their cultural organizations and activities. Yiddish newspapers, theatres, clubs, etc., were organized and flourished. These at first served to widen the breach between the two groups. The newspapers constantly criticized the "uptowners," or the German Jews, because of their attitude toward the "downtowners," and their ways of keeping them. This criticism and fault-finding were resented by the older settlers. Nor were the cultural activities and their expressions looked upon with favor. Rather were they considered an attempt on the part of the recent arrivals to recreate or transplant their old-world conditions of life.[280] It was only the need for alleviating the sufferings of the Jews overseas during the World War, that brought the two groups together for a common effort. But the old differences and animosities are still in existence although they are no longer on the surface.

D. Programs of Jewish Adjustment

The earlier problem of adjusting the Jewish immigrant to American life has its counterpart in the larger and ever-present problem of Jewish adjustment in America. Although, as we have seen, the problems of economic adjustment are by no means solved and may in fact be said to be assuming increasing importance and severity, (See pages 36) the problems of social and cultural adjustment are much more serious. Various programs and solutions have been advanced. Each has its own adherents who endeavor to foster it and to convince a skeptical or indifferent public to its virtues and advantages over the others. It is impossible to classify and define them so that the programs and definitions would be mutually exclusive. Each of the proposed solutions has elements in common with the others. All that can be attempted here, therefore, is a somewhat arbitrary grouping for purposes of brief exposition and clarification.

The problem basic to all programs of Jewish adjustment in the United States is that of Jewish survival. Should the Jews continue to maintain their identity and if so what aspects of their life and characteristics as Jews differentiate them from the rest of the population, and which of these should be cultivated and perpetuated? These are the questions which each program for Jewish adjustment is endeavoring to answer. Three programs and groups are distinguishable on the basis of their attitude toward the problem of Jewish survival. They are: 1. The Religionists; 2. The Culturists; and 3. The Assimliationists.

Before considering these three viewpoints and their implications it should be pointed out that although it seems necessary to speak of "groups," in this connection, it is not intended to imply that they are either clearly defined or well organized, except in a few instances. Nor should it be inferred that all American Jews are divided according to the three programs mentioned. It is much more likely that the vast majority are only vaguely aware of the conflicting views and their significance. Nevertheless, these philosophies and the corresponding programs for their implimentation, rightly understood, are the key to an understanding of organized Jewish life in the United States.

1. *The Religionists.*—This term is used to designate those who hold that the Jewish religion is the distinguishing and determining characteristic of Jews in their individual and group life. According to them, it is the Jewish religion, or Judaism, that has kept the Jews apart from tke rest of the world. It is Judaism that is the distinctive Jewish contribution to civilization and enabled them to withstand their sufferings and numberless persecutions. It is this Judaism that Jews should foster, maintain and

preserve. In most other aspects, such as economics, politics, the arts, etc., Jews should merge with the rest of the populations among whom they live. So long as one adheres to the Jewish religion, be he a strictly observing Orthodox Jew or a less strict Conservative Jew, or a Reform Jew who pays little heed to the traditional practices and observances, he is a Jew.

Many Orthodox, Conservative, and Reform Jews who may otherwise have little in common, subscribe to this view. One may find among its adherents the immigrant from Eastern Europe, who came directly from a ghetto environment, who had little or no secular education or educational opportunity, who is totally unaware of biblical criticism and who thinks of Jewish life and its problems in terms similar to those characteristic of Jewish life in the Middle Ages. One may also find among its adherents Conservative and Reform Jews whose forebears lived in the United States for hundreds of years, who had the best educational opportunities and advantages, who honor Jewish traditional practices by indifference rather than observance, who more nearly resemble their Christian neighbors in dress, manner, interests, culture and world outlook, than their East-European coreligionists.

The Religionists may be nationalists, non-nationalists, or anti-nationalists in their attitude toward Jewish survival and the world Jewish problem. Indeed, all three views are found among them. They tend to affiliate in their communal activity in accordance with their attitude toward nationalism. The nationalists, whether Reform, Conservative, or Orthodox, will most likely identify themselves with some organization working for the upbuilding of Palestine or for the removal of Jewish discrimination in this and other countries, with a nationalist orientation.

The non-nationalists and anti-nationalists may or may not be affiliated with Palestinian enterprises. If they are, such affiliation is likely to be tenuous. The non-nationalists, and occasionally even the anti-nationalists, may contribute toward some non-political Zionist organizations, such as the Jewish National Fund for the purchase of land, the Hebrew University, the Palestine Economic Corporation, or Hadassah, the Women's Zionist Organization, because of its social service program. Some of them are members of the Jewish Agency for Palestine through its Non-Zionist division, and contribute toward the Palestine Foundation Fund (*Keren Hayesod*) despite the fact that this fund covers the entire budget of the Jewish Agency, including political work to which they may be opposed.

But such contribution is made, especially in the case of the anti-nationalists, because of convenience or necessity due to the united campaigns for Palestine and other overseas and national needs. (See page 127). It is rarely made out of conviction or love for Palestine as is the case with Zionists and nationalists. Nor is it made, except in rare instances, because of a great urge to create in Palestine a spiritual center for the Jews in the Diaspora. Most of them do not think that they are in the Diaspora, in the sense in which many nationalists use this term, and con-

sider themselves perfectly at home in the United States.
Palestine has little emotional or logical hold upon them if
they are Reformed, and has only a nostalgic, mystical and
sentimental but no political or practical appeal for them if
Orthodox.

They usually seek other outlets and affiliations for the
satisfaction of such urge as they may feel to be active in
Jewish group effort. These they find, in most instances,
if they are Orthodox, in their religious organizations and
related efforts; if Reform, they will most likely find their
opportunity in the various philanthropic and protective
organizations for local, national and overseas problems.
They are also active in their Synagogue or Temple groups,
many believing that the Temple or Synagogue should be
the center of Jewish communal activity. Intense as may
be the efforts of the Reformed along these lines and closely
identified as they are with the Jewish group through such
activity and Temple affiliation, it is frequently difficult
and sometimes impossible to distinguish between them
and those who are frankly assimilationist, so far as their
practical work is concerned.

One of the most important criticisms leveled against
the Religionist program is that it leaves little or no room
for Jews who are openly irreligious or anti-religious and
who are, nevertheless, deeply interested in Jewish welfare
and are closely affiliated with Jewish organizations giving
of their time, money, and energy toward the alleviation
of Jewish suffering wherever it may be found. Many Religionists have little respect or use for such persons as Jews.[28d]

2. *The Culturists.*—It is even more difficult accurately to characterize the Culturists. While they have some elements in common they also differ in many ways. Among the most important principles they hold in common is their belief in Jewish survival and the development and perpetuation of Jewish culture. But there is little agreement on the nature of this culture, the means for its perpetuation, the place of religion, Jewish nationalism, the causes and cures of anti-Semitism, economic programs, etc.

Most of the Culturists approach the problem of Jewish survival quite independently of the Jewish religion. Even those who ascribe an important place to religion in Jewish life, view it as only one phase, although perhaps the most important single aspect, of Jewish culture. The most representative among those who hold this view are the Reconstructionists. Others would completely secularize Jewish life and exclude the religious element from the culture they wish to foster and develop. They all subscribe to the theory of cultural pluralism as the basis for Jewish adjustment in America. They maintain that the American culture, which is still in the making, is a product of many older cultures. Hence they believe that America should encourage the different cultural groups to express themselves in terms of their own cultures. They believe further, that the Jews can make their best contribution to their own development and to the development of American civilization by emphasizing and perpetuating their own cultural institutions. Accordingly they are inclined to stress the importance of the "Jewish Community" although they may be out of sympathy with the existing forms of Jewish community organization and are opposed to current practices and leadership.

In orientation toward the world Jewish problem the adherents to this point of view can be divided, like the Religionists, into nationalists of various hues, non-nationalists, and anti-nationalists. The nationalists, of the Zionist variety, look upon the Jews as a people, or a nation, whose greatest need is the development of a national home in Palestine which should be a cultural center for the Jews throughout the world, and a political homeland for those who should wish to settle there. They are among the hardest workers for Palestine and are Hebraists in sympathy. They have influenced the *Talmud Torahs* and Hebrew schools where their children receive their Jewish education in Hebrew and are brought up to appreciate their people, revere its past, and work for its future. They are also taught to love the Hebrew language and literature, through which they can best absorb the priceless heritage left them by their ancient prophets, poets, and philosophers.

Others, including some of the non-nationalists and anti-nationalists, believe that the Yiddish language and literature are the best if not exclusive media for the expression of the Jewish genius. The more enterprising among them built Yiddish schools for the purpose of transmitting to their children this type of Jewish heritage and developing in them an appreciation of the Yiddish language and literature. Some extremists among them would go so far as to

demand official recognition as a minority group in the
United States, with Yiddish as its medium of expression.
Most of these are violently opposed to Zionism. These
Yiddishists are chiefly of the laboring group, with a trade-
union or socialist outlook, although there is a considerable admixture of middle class and white collar occupations among them.

Religiously, the Yiddishists are usually inclined toward
indifference or agnosticism, while the Zionists and Hebraists, especially those of the Reconstructionist viewpoint,
are likely to be fairly strict observers of the traditional
and religious practices. This is not so much because they
believe that these observances are of divine origin as
because they are part of the heritage of the Jewish people
and to observe them is to identify oneself with one's people.
(See page 46). The Labor Zionists represent a synthesis
between Zionism, Yiddishism and Socialism, although
they would grant exclusive right to the Hebrew language
in Palestine and feature it as a subject of instruction in
their schools in the United States.

They also present a wide divergence in views as to the
social and economic system in the United States best
suited for the fostering of the respective schemes of Jewish
life. There is no Fascist or Totalitarian group within the
Jewish community. There exists a very small but extremely
vocal group of revolutionary Socialists and Communists.
The Labor Zionists, some Reconstructionists, and many
of the Yiddishists, are inclined to favor a collectivist society
in the United States, to be achieved by reforming the

present society through evolutionary and democratic means. The vast majority of American Jews see their future as inextricably interwoven with the welfare of the rest of the population and are, therefore, passionate believers in democracy, law, and order.[28e]

3. *The Assimilationists.*—In this category are grouped those who have no interest in Jewish survival, and who hold, on the contrary, that the Jews are doomed to extinction through the process of assimilation which is constantly going on. This process, they believe, should be encouraged, and cannot and should not be stopped. Some of the moderates among them may believe that it should be retarded. But even they view assimilation as desirable and inevitable.

The adherents of this view find it very difficult and frequently impossible to be consistent with respect to their beliefs and practices. Many of them are among the most active lay and professional workers in the Jewish communal institutions and agencies, despite their belief that Jewish communal activity makes for separatism, intolerance, creates anti-Semitism, and should therefore be discouraged. They give of their time, energy, and substance to the development of Jewish community activities, including Jewish education, although they look upon it as alien to American life and as handicapping the children receiving such an education. Some of them contribute to the upbuilding of Palestine for the same reasons as do some of the other anti-nationalists, although they are opposed to Palestine as a Jewish State, or as a Jewish National Home, or even as a cultural center except possibly as a place of refuge for the persecuted Jews who may wish to go there. They would encourage assimilationist programs although, when pressed, they admit that assimilation is unworkable as a practical program for the masses especially since the German-Jewish tragedy. In their economic and political philosophy they are usually either extremely conservative or reactionary if they are wealthy, or they may be among the most radical Marxists if they are among the workers. Some are members of temples; others may be atheists or agnostics.[281] Well meaning and hard working as they may be, there can be little doubt that they exercise a negative influence on Jewish communal life. Their aim and philosophy, if successful, could lead only to Jewish community disintegration. (See pages 140–148).

As has been pointed out in the beginning of this discussion, there are many Jews who take their Jewishness for granted and think little upon the problem of Jewish survival and the controversies suggested above. Perhaps the vast majority are to be found in this category.

CHAPTER V

COMMUNAL ORGANIZATIONS FOR RELIGIOUS ACTIVITIES, EDUCATION AND CIVIC PROTECTION

A. Religious Activities

At first glance it appears as if chaos reigns in religious activities in the Jewish communities in the United States. Such, however, is not actually the case. Roughly speaking, observant Jews in the United States may be divided into three groups with respect to religious affiliation and practice. In the ascending order of their numerical strength they are as follows: (1) Reform Jews, those who are members of reform temples where services have departed substantially from the traditional orthodox service, men and women sitting side by side, the men with bare heads, with mixed choirs and organ music, and among whom Sabbath observance is the exception rather than the rule. Some of these temples hold their services on Sundays in an effort to attract the men who are usually in business on Saturday. (2) The Conservative Group, those who have departed in some measure from the traditional services but have not gone to the extent of the Reformed. One section of this group, now being referred to as the "Reconstructionists," revere traditional practices not so much because they are commanded by God, but because they are part of the Jewish folkways and *mores*, and hold that to adhere to them is to indicate one's connection with the

Jewish people. (3) The third group consists of the Orthodox, those who adhere strictly to the traditional faith and forms of observance.

There are a number of Jews in this country who have no particular religious affiliation during the entire year. During the High Holy Days many attend the existing synagogues and temples by purchasing seats for the occasion, while others attend services in improvised synagogues usually located in public meeting places and, occasionally, even in dance halls, rented for the period and the occasion as commercial ventures by individuals and organizations. The people attending these services are mostly Orthodox in background. Many of the religiously unaffiliated Jews use other means of identification with the Jewish people, such as membership in charitable organizations, cultural clubs, fraternal organizations, etc., and affiliation with Zionism or other Jewish movements.

In each of these groups may be found a large variety of divergent views, practices and forms of religious observance. The lines of demarcation between them are not always sharp and are at best arbitrary.

It is not definitely known how many synagogues, temples and other houses of worship there are in the United States. It is estimated that The Union of American Hebrew Congregations, representing the reform or liberal group, has approximately 290 temples, with a total membership of about 50,000. The temple brotherhoods, subsidiary organization of the Union, have a total membership of approximately 20,000. The temple sisterhoods, of which there are

about 350, have a total membership of about 70,000. The
Union spends approximately one-half million dollars on its
activities. This includes the budget of the Hebrew Union
College, which trains reform Rabbis.[29]

The United Synagogue of America represents the conservative group. Approximately 250 synagogues affiliated
with this organization, and about the same number of unaffiliated synagogues, have a total membership of about 75,000.
It has a Women's League comprising 280 organizations,
with a total membership of about 40,000. Its Brotherhoods
have about 100 individual organizations with a total membership of about 10,000. There are approximately 250 organizations in its Young People's League, which is the youth
organization, with a total membership of about 30,000.[30]

The Orthodox groups are not nearly as well organized
as are the other two, although they, too, have a central
organization, The Union of Orthodox Jewish Congregations.
It is almost impossible to get any definite information with
respect to either the number of synagogues or their memberships. Moreover, they are much less united with respect
to policy of religious observance and practice. Thus, whereas
each of the other two groups has a central organization,
with its representative rabbinical seminary and rabbinical
conference, the Orthodox group has several seminaries and
several rabbinical conferences.

There is no safe way of estimating the number of Jewish
individuals who are affiliated with synagogues. On the
basis of the above figures it might be said that no more
than between 300,000 and 350,000 men and women are

directly and actively connected with synagogues. However, since a member is usually the head of the family and the other members are assumed to have affiliation by virtue of such membership, it may be said that between 1,000,000 and 1,500,000 are associated with religious organizations and activity.

It should be added that a study of Jewish Congregations in the United States, made in 1927, showed that there were 3,118 permanent congregations in the U. S. The total membership was not reported, but 1,290 congregations reported a total expenditure during the previous fiscal year of $18,-001,771. Also, 2,348 of the congregations reported the total value of their buildings was $155,744,666.[31] This is by no means the total expenditure for religious activity by the Jews in the United States.

Each of the three groups mentioned above, carries on its educational activities through its central organization. The Union of American Hebrew Congregations conducts educational activities of a national and local type. It has a close relationship with the Hebrew Union College which trains the reform rabbis, who have an organization of their own, the Central Conference of American Rabbis. It has a comparatively large organization for educational purposes in and outside of the temples, including preparation of text books for the Sunday Schools, Regional Conferences, stimulation of their temple brotherhoods and sisterhoods, etc. The United Synagogue of America performs similar functions for the conservative group, with the Jewish Theological Seminary of America as the educational institution for training conservative Rabbis, whose alumni are organized in the Rabbinical Assembly of America. The Union of Orthodox Jewish Congregations of America aims to perform the same services with the limitations noted above. Though not as intimately related to the organization, the Yeshiva College and the Isaac Elchanan Seminary trains Rabbis for this group. There are several other seminaries for training Orthodox Rabbis.

There is another, independent institution for the training of liberal Rabbis, The Jewish Institute of Religion in New York City.

There are no central funds for maintaining religious institutions whether synagogues or seminaries. The former are usually supported by membership fees and donations of members; the latter, by endowment funds and special gifts. Each synagogue, able to afford it, usually maintains its own rabbi. Smaller communities sometimes have itinerant rabbis who conduct services and perform other rabbinical functions as necessary. Some of the very small communities have one person who serves in the capacity of rabbi, *shohet* (one who is empowered to perform the ritual slaughter of cattle and poultry), *mohel* (one who is authorized to perform the religious rite of circumcision), and Hebrew teacher.

Some rabbis have created for themselves positions of outstanding leadership in their respective communities. In general, it may be said that the synagogue looks to the Rabbi to be not only its spiritual guide and to superintend the religious education of the children, to administer the affairs of the congregation, and to conduct the necessary rabbinical functions at births, marriages, deaths, etc., but to be its representative in the general community. Rabbis are, therefore, prominent in civic, religious, philanthropic, and other communal affairs, Jewish and non-Jewish. In a number of instances, rabbis have taken leading parts in social reform movements in their respective communities.

B. Education

1. *Secular Education.*—The Jews in the United States send their children to the public elementary, secondary and higher schools. There are comparatively few Jewish parochial schools. In this way, Jewish children are trained from an early date to feel at home with their non-Jewish neighbors and are brought up to full participation in American cultural life. As indicated elsewhere, the Jews have a relatively high proportion of attendance in all educational institutions, from the elementary school to the university and technical and professional schools.

The Youth Study in New York City already referred to (page 5 ff.) contained some interesting data about the education of Jews which are summarized in Table 16. According to this study only a negligible number of Jews (about 2%) fail to complete elementary school as compared to 11 per cent of non-Jews. Almost twice as many Jews as non-Jews complete high school. About four times as many Jewish males, and approximately three times as many Jewish females, complete college and go on to graduate study, as do the respective non-Jewish youth.

TABLE 16

DISTRIBUTION OF JEWISH AND NON-JEWISH YOUTH IN
NEW YORK CITY BY TYPE AND AMOUNT OF
EDUCATION RECEIVED

(Based on a study of every hundredth family)

Grade in School at time of leaving	Jewish		Non-Jewish	
	Male	Female	Male	Female
Before completing 8th grade....	1.7	2.1	11.7	10.0
Before completing high school...	52.5	53.0	69.3	69.8
Completed high school.........	22.9	33.7	13.5	16.0
Before completing college.......	16.0	7.4	3.9	2.7
Completed college and some graduate study..............	6.9	3.8	1.6	1.5

A study, recently published by the B'nai B'rith, of the
Jewish students in 1319 colleges and universities throughout
the land, shows that of 1,148,393 students, 104,906, or
9.13%, are Jews. In other words, the Jewish population
which constitutes 3.58% of the general population, con-
tributes 9.13% of the students in the higher educational
institutions. The Jewish students range from 1.2% in the
mountain states to 49.6% in New York City, where the
Jewish population is 29.6% of the total population.[32]

There are no universities, technical or professional schools,
outside of several seminaries, a college for Hebrew and
cognate learning, and a school for social workers, under
Jewish auspices.[33] Various attempts have been made from
time to time to encourage the organization of such institutions but they have always met with such resistance that
nothing came of them. About ten years ago the Yeshiva
College was organized. But this is closely connected with
the Orthodox Seminary and is in reality a parochial school.

2. *Jewish Education.*—Jewish education was always more
or less informal, was always partly affiliated with the synagogue, and was always considered a responsibility of the
community. The attitude of Jewish parents toward the
education of their children, particularly their male children,
is well known. *Talmud Torahs* were among the most favored
organizations in the Jewish community and the education
of poor children was considered a primary obligation on
each community from time immemorial.[34] In this country
the traditional attitudes toward Jewish education, more or
less religious, developed the traditional types of Jewish
educational institutions, such as the *Talmud Torah* (a communal Hebrew School originally intended for poor children),
and the *Heder* (a private Hebrew School). With the development of the public school and with compulsory universal
education, the *Talmud Torah* and the traditional private
teacher were seriously challenged. The dissatisfactions with
these institutions were responsible, in part, for the creation
of Sunday Schools connected with the synagogues. It became the practice of each reform temple and, later, of the
more progressive conservative synagogues, to maintain
schools which held classes on Sunday mornings for the
religious education of the children whose parents were members of the congregations. Opinions differ as to the effec-
tiveness of these schools, of which there are large numbers
in the United States and which provide some kind of Jewish
education for children who might otherwise receive none.
It was not until 1910 that a movement, sponsored by a
small group under the leadership of a few idealists, developed

a modern Jewish educational program. This development was at a very rapid pace, so that practically every one of the larger Jewish communities had a fairly comprehensive program of Jewish education by the end of the third decade of the present century. As a result of this movement, the old Hebrew School and *Talmud Torah*, frequently located in dingy, dark, unattractive quarters, gave way, in many instances, to modern schools, located in attractive, airy and sunny rooms, with college-trained men and women as teachers, with a curriculum which aims at transmitting to the pupils the Jewish cultural heritage.[35]

These systems of Jewish education in the larger communities are usually part of the Federations of Jewish Charities. They are aided by boards of Jewish education which supervise and finance, in part or in whole, the Jewish educational institutions which aim to provide at least a minimum of Jewish education for Jewish youth. Hebrew schools, Hebrew high schools, teachers institutes, and colleges of Jewish studies, sprang up in the different communities. The old type *Melamed* (Hebrew teacher) is rapidly passing from the scene. Men and women born and educated in America, graduates of American colleges and universities, with graduate work in the best teachers colleges and universities, entered the classrooms and became the supervisors of the Jewish educational systems. A resurgence of, and a revival of interest in, Jewish education made themselves felt throughout the country and permeated the Jewish communities and Jewish community activity. Like every revival movement it has its friends and enemies. Some see in it a deviation from orthodox forms and practices and are, therefore, opposed to it. Others see in it an intensification of Jewish life which seems to them opposed to Americanization as they conceive it. They, too, are opposed to it. Between these two extremes, is a group of persons, usually the conservative elements in the Jewish community, who look upon it as a worthwhile movement from which will emerge the type of Jewish education best adapted to the American scene and which will meet the needs of American Jewry.

There is no exact information as to how many Jewish children receive a Jewish education. Estimates vary from 20% to 40%. A recent study,[36] indicates that of 800,000 Jewish children of school age, only 25% attend Jewish schools at any one time. Of these, 55% attend week-day schools; 37.5% attend Sunday Schools; 6% attend private week-day schools; 1.5% attend parochial schools. The same authority estimates that approximately $5,825,000 is spent annually on Jewish education. Of this sum, about 71% comes from tuition fees; 17% comes from local philanthropic funds, such as Federations of Jewish Charities; 12% from central communal, national, or Seminary funds. A different study estimates that about one-third of the children enrolled continue until graduation.[37]

The problems facing Jewish education in this country are: (1) inadequate funds, it having been estimated that adequate Jewish education would require almost as much money as all the other Jewish communal activities put together; (2) lack of time, since most of the pupils attend the public schools and there is very little time or energy left for Jewish education; (3) suitable curricula; (4) lack of a real and sustained interest on the part of leaders and parents in a comprehensive Jewish educational program; (5) lack of a universally acceptable philosophy as to the aim and content of Jewish education in the United States; (6) congregational vs. communal control and organization; (7) standards of education, minimum remuneration, and tenure for teachers.[38]

There are a number of institutions throughout the country for training teachers for the Jewish schools. Usually each large community has its own teacher-training school. The best known of these are the schools located in New York City, Boston, and Chicago. There exists a National Council for Jewish Education made up of the leaders of the Jewish educational movement throughout the country which issues *Jewish Education*, a quarterly journal, and which holds annual meetings for the discussion of common problems. There are also several organizations of Jewish teachers and principals, somewhat in the nature of trade unions.

One very interesting enterprise in Jewish education is that comprising the Yiddish schools for children. The language of instruction is Yiddish and the point of view is liberal; in many instances, socialistic. They aim at training the children in what they term the language of their parents. This movement is about three decades old and has a great many useful and worthwhile achievements to its credit. It is estimated that there are more than 300 Yiddish schools in the United States and that they have a total enrollment of 21,000 children.[39]

The depression, with the consequent shortage of funds
and the urge to reduce expenditures where possible, has
tended to focus attention and criticism upon the Jewish
education movement as one of the non-essentials and not
belonging by right to the Jewish community as represented
by the Federation of Jewish Charities. This is the situation
in which Jewish education finds itself at the present time.
Its progress has been halted. In many instances it has lost
ground. Whether it will recapture its position, whether it
will continue to develop along its former lines and rate of
progress, only the future can tell.[40]

C. Civic Protection

There are four organizations in the United States con-
cerned with the problem of protection of Jewish rights in
this country and abroad. They are: The American Jewish
Committee, The American Jewish Congress, The Anti-
Defamation League of the B'nai B'rith, and The Jewish
Labor Committee.

The American Jewish Committee was organized in 1906
with the avowed purpose "to safeguard the civil and religious
rights of Jews, to combat discrimination and allay prejudice, to aid victims of persecution and calamity." Its
activities cover all countries where Jews reside and where
there are evidences of anti-Semitic activities. A large
portion of its efforts are devoted to the dissemination of
educational literature, aiming to combat anti-Semitism in
the United States. More recently, its major activities have
been concerned with exposing Nazi propaganda in this

country and elsewhere and fighting anti-Jewish discrimination here. Because of its many and varied contacts with government officials here and abroad, as well as with civic organizations, individuals and religious bodies in other countries, it is enabled to carry on an effective world-wide activity. Its publications are widely distributed and it exercises important influence directly and indirectly on public opinion in this country and elsewhere. While in its Jewish orientation it is anti-nationalistic, it is definitely pro-Palestine. Some of its most prominent leaders are also leading non-Zionist members of the Jewish Agency for Palestine. The Committee as such is pledged to cooperate "with those who, attracted by religious or historic association, shall seek to establish in Palestine a center for Judaism, for the stimulation of our faith, for the pursuit and development of literature, science and art in a Jewish environment, and for the rehabilitation of the land."[41] Its financial support comes mainly from its members, donations, and appropriations from federations and welfare funds throughout the country.

The American Jewish Congress, a successor to an earlier body of the same name, was organized in 1922. The first American Jewish Congress was organized in 1917 for the purpose of naming a commission to the Peace Conference at Versailles. That Congress was a temporary body with which the American Jewish Committee and other national organizations were affiliated. It was set up on the basis of a written agreement which provided that it should go out of existence after the Peace Treaty was signed. Its commission played an important role in bringing about the inclusion of the minority rights clauses in the peace treaties. This Congress adjourned *sine die* in 1920, in accordance with the written agreement reached before the Congress was convened, and after accepting the report of the commission which had been sent to the Peace Conference.

It was not until two years later that the present Congress was organized. Although its leaders claim that it is a "democratic organization," there is no record of a popular or democratic election since its organization.[42] Its purposes are practically the same as those of the American Jewish Committee, except that, in its aims at dealing with the civic, political, economic and religious rights of the Jews in all lands, it is nationalistically motivated. Some of its leaders are also the most prominent leaders in Zionist activities. They are also the leaders in the World Jewish Congress movement. In general its form of organization is similar to that of the American Jewish Committee. It also has an executive committee and various other standing committees. However, there are branches of the Congress in a number of cities in the United States. It differs fundamentally from the American Jewish Committee in sponsoring mass activities, such as protests against the present German government, a boycott against German-made goods, and mass meetings. Its funds come from its members, and from federations and welfare funds.

The B'nai B'rith, a fraternal organization with branches throughout the world, carries on its program of civic protection largely through its Anti-Defamation League. This League was organized in 1913 for the purpose of stimulating good-will and combating anti-Semitism. The League has concentrated its activities on watching the press, the stage, the screen, radio, school texts, etc. It carries on an educational program through the dissemination of books and pamphlets, and by providing speakers for suitable occasions. The income of the Anti-Defamation League comes from the exchequer of the B'nai B'rith, which in turn receives its income from membership fees. More recently because of its intensified activity and enlarged program, the B'nai B'rith has undertaken wider campaigns for funds. It also receives funds from the federations and welfare funds.[43]

The Jewish Labor Committee, organized only in 1934, has in general the same purposes as the other three organizations. However, it differs from the others in its orientation and in its approach. Because of its contacts and affiliations with labor organizations, more particularly the American Federation of Labor, it has been helpful in furthering and effectuating the anti-Nazi boycott. It is maintained with funds coming from its membership and central labor organizations.[44]

These four organizations, though having practically the same purpose, are responsible to different sections in the community, although there is some overlapping in the memberships. In general it may be said that the American Jewish Committee, made up as it is of the upper economic strata of the Jewish population, is responsible to them for its policies and procedures. The American Jewish Congress is made up very largely of representatives of the middle class and is responsible to them for its activities. The B'nai B'rith is composed mainly of the middle class and professional group and its policies are set by them. The Jewish Labor Committee has its own constituency. It is safe to say, therefore, that whereas the four organizations together probably constitute a cross-section of the entire Jewish population in the United States, no one organization is completely or fully representative.

The differences in orientation and methods of work which characterize these organizations give rise to frequent conflicts which, in the opinion of many, weaken the Jewish community. Demands are heard from time to time for unity or at least a united front.[45] Many are of the opinion, however, that unity is neither possible nor desirable. There is a Joint Consultative Council made up of representatives from the different organizations, which discusses common problems and endeavors to formulate common procedures. In some instances, where all organizations cannot agree on a common policy, two or more may unite.

Mention should perhaps also be made here of two additional protective organizations. One of these is the Non-Sectarian Anti-Nazi League, of which a number of Jewish organizations and individuals are members. The other is a Jewish protective organization maintained by the Communist Party. But neither of these two organizations has the standing in the Jewish community that the other four have attained.

CHAPTER VI

ORGANIZATIONS FOR THE CARE OF THE NEEDY, THE SICK, DEPENDENT CHILDREN, AND THE AGED

Before proceeding to discuss the different types of organizations functioning in the Jewish community in the social service sphere, it may be well to obtain a bird's-eye view of the extent and cost of these activities.

It has been estimated that there are more than 4,000 communal agencies receiving financial support from central funds. These agencies spend approximately $50,000,000 annually in serving the sick; the poor; the widows; orphans; the maladjusted; the educational, cultural and recreational needs; needy Jews overseas; and the upbuilding of Palestine. Table 17 presents a distribution of these expenditures. It will be observed that about 85% is spent by agencies serving the needs in their respective localities or communities; about 5% is spent by national or regional agencies in this country; about 7% is spent by overseas agencies and 2½% is spent in the administration of the agencies which raise these large sums.

If to this sum of close to $50,000,000 is added the sum spent for religious activities (See page 54), and the sums spent for organizations and activities which are maintained by more restricted groups such as the unaffiliated societies, fraternal organizations, *landsmanschaften*, cultural agencies, etc., it is not too much to say that the Jewish people in the

67

TABLE 17

EXPENDITURES OF LOCAL, NATIONAL AND OVERSEAS
JEWISH SOCIAL AGENCIES IN 1935[46]

Field and Type of Service	Number of Agencies	Disbursements	
		Amount	Per cent
1. Local and Regional Agencies			
Health..........................	67	$18,786,222	39.0
Family Service and Relief.........	113	4,179,713	8.7
Child Welfare....................	94	5,422,521	11.2
Care of Aged....................	60	2,322,609	4.8
Service to Homeless and Unattached.	15	93,677	0.2
Employment and Vocational Guidance...........................	10	237,516	0.5
Remedial Loans..................	12	89,796	0.2
Vacation Service.................	22	270,323	0.6
Centers and Settlements...........	216	4,000,000	8.3
Jewish Education.................	2,200	5,825,000	12.1
Total for Local Agencies........	3,909	$41,227,377	85.6
2. National Agencies...................	26	2,477,673	5.1
3. Overseas Agencies..................	11	3,251,988	6.8
4. Administration of Federations and Welfare Funds, Fund Raising, etc........	89	1,200,000	2.5
Total......................	4.035	$48,157,038	100.0

United States spend close to $100,000,000 each year on organizations and activities to serve their social, religious and educational needs.

With this introduction, we can now turn to a consideration of the more formal types of organizations which have been created to meet these needs. Before doing so, however, it may be well to explain that the more extensive discussion including the historical background in the section immediately following, that on poverty and dependency, is due to the belief that this type of social work is typical of and basic to the others. This is the reason also for the more detailed discussion of the problems faced by the family agencies in the sections on trends and tendencies (pp. 107ff.).

For the same reason emphasis is laid on the developments in New York City. It would make the treatment much too complex and confusing if the developments in the other cities were to be described in any reasonable detail.

A. Poverty and Dependency

Great progress has been made in provisions for the care of the poor in the Jewish communities of the United States. There are many organizations, usually referred to as "family care agencies," for aiding Jewish families and individuals who need financial and other types of assistance in order to maintain themselves or reacquire an independent status. This type of social service, with health, and child care, to be discussed later, frequently required the major portion of the funds collected by the federations of Jewish charities. So that this field of Jewish social work in the United States may be viewed in its proper perspective, and may serve as an introduction to the other fields to be discussed, it is necessary to review briefly some of the traditional attitudes among Jews regarding the care of the poor and needy which gave rise to this development.

The thoughtful and considerate care of the poor has ever been foremost in the attention of Jewish communities and their leaders throughout the ages. As a result of the attitudes in the Bible and the forms and practices of charity outlined in the Talmud,[47] institutions and practices grew up in the Jewish communities which left an indelible imprint upon the Jew regarding his responsibility for his less fortunate brother. Charity became a living guide to one's relation to his fellow man and permeated and controlled one's daily life. In the Codifications, which are still the guides to Jewish social and religious practices with large portions of the Jewish population, charity and charitable acts hold a most important place. The Code of Maimonides, who lived in the 12th and 13th centuries, gives an interesting series of grades or values in charitable giving. The first and lowest degree of charity consists of giving to the poor but only after much pressure; the second is giving in a kindly spirit but less than one's means allow; the third consists of giving directly to the poor after being solicited; the fourth is giving before one is asked and directly to the poor; the fifth, when the donor does not know the recipient but the recipient knows the donor; the sixth grade is when the donor knows the recipient but the latter does not know the donor; the seventh is that type of giving which makes it impossible for the donor to know the recipient or the recipient the donor; the eighth and highest type of charity is that which enables the poor to become self-supporting either through loans or business establishment or finding employment. Jewish social agencies in America today, though perhaps unconsciously, are striving to live up to the highest of the eight grades of charity. The self-support departments of family care agencies, which enable dependent families to become self-supporting through the purchase of businesses of various types, are clearly engaging in the highest type of charity;[48] Federations which make it impossible for the donor and recipient to know each other act strictly in accord, though perhaps for entirely different reasons, with the principles of sound philanthropic practice laid down by the famous Jewish philosopher more than seven hundred years ago.

In addition to this very rich and compelling background of Jewish charitable practice, there grew up the feeling on the part of the Jews throughout the ages that the welfare of the group is inextricably interwoven with the welfare of the individual. This was especially borne in on them during the Middle Ages when, because of persecutions, expulsions, and discriminations, it became necessary for the Jewish communities and individuals to protect other Jews in so far as possible. Jewish communities had to prepare themselves as best they could to receive wandering Jews. Shelters had to be established and arrangements made for meeting all of the other needs of the wanderers, since the Jewish poor could neither apply for nor receive aid from the general community. The self-government of the Jewish group also necessitated communal provisions for the complete care of the needy so that the seven branches of Jewish charity mentioned in the Rabbinic literature were, and still are, fully provided for. These are: feeding the hungry, clothing the naked, visiting the sick, burying the dead and comforting the mourners, redeeming the captives, educating the fatherless and sheltering the homeless, and providing poor maidens with dowries.

It would be difficult to over-emphasize the importance which the Jewish communities during the Middle Ages attached to the care of the poor, the orphan, the stranger and the captive. The Biblical and Talmudic admonitions were observed in spirit and letter with the utmost scrupulousness.

Communities vied with each other in the generosity which they showered upon some of these unfortunates. To be an orphan or a widow was to be in a privileged position in the Jewish community. For they stood, in accordance with the Biblical teachings, under the special protection of God, Himself. The foremost Jewish humorist, Sholem Aleichem, who described Jewish life with rare skill and insight, epitomized the attitude of the Jew toward the orphan by beginning one of his most important books with the statement, "I am lucky, I am an orphan." No less kind was the Jewish community to the Jewish wanderer. The age-old custom of a "guest for the Sabbath" typifies the attitude in this regard. These attitudes and practices take on special significance when they are compared with the practices among non-Jews of the same and later periods. Compare, for instance, the degrees of charity of Maimonides and the solicitude of the Jewish community for the welfare of wanderers, with the English Poor Law which, in the middle of the sixteenth century, punished wanderers and vagabonds by branding them with the letter "V," assigned them as slaves to those who would claim them, fed them with "bread and water and refuse meat," branded them with the letter "S" on the cheek and enslaved them for life if they escaped during the first year, and put them to death as felons if they escaped again![49]

It was the practice in Jewish communities, from time immemorial, for the best and most prominent people to interest themselves in charitable activities. Josephus tells us that, in the first century, when Palestine was stricken

with a famine, Queen Helena of Adiabene sent shiploads
of food to the foremost men of Jerusalem so that they might
distribute it among the people. During the Middle Ages,
only the very finest members of the Jewish community were
selected as "gabbaei tsedakah" or overseers of the poor.
So honored were these latter that a son of such an overseer
was eligible to marry into a priestly family without the
usual inquiry as to the purity of his descent.[50]

This was the background for the development of Jewish
philanthropy in the United States. Traditional practices
of two thousand years were transported to these shores and
became no less a part of the social practices of the early
Jewish settlers on the new continent than they were in the
Old World. In addition to this traditional heritage was
the realization from the very beginning of Jewish sojourn
in the new land, that the responsibility of Jew for Jew was
to hold true no less here than in European countries. The
very first group of Jews that settled in New Netherlands
in 1654, the twenty-seven persons who came here on the
"St. Charles," found that several of their number were
to be held as hostages for the payment of passage by the
rest of them. Similarly, the unwillingness of Governor
Stuyvesant of New Amsterdam (now New York City), to
let them remain here was directed not against any one of
them but against the entire group. (It may be worth mentioning in this connection that the common belief, which
has been frequently cited as the reason for the existence of
separate Jewish charities in the United States, that these
early settlers promised to take care of their own poor as a

condition for being permitted to remain, is not quite true. Although the Dutch West India Co. named such a condition, there is no evidence that Stuyvesant tried to impose it or that the Jewish settlers accepted it.)[51] When one fought for rights and won them, they were won for the group, even as discriminations against one tended to become practices against all.

It may be doubted, however, whether Jewish philanthropy would have developed as it has in the United States if there had not been the enormous increase in population during the nineteenth century. As we have seen, it has been estimated that by 1825 there were approximately only 6,000 Jews in the United States. In the following century the population grew to almost four and one-half million, an increase of over 700%. This increase was largely due to immigration, mainly from Germany between 1825 and 1880, and from East-European countries between 1880 and 1925.

The hundreds of thousands of immigrants since 1880 made it necessary for the earlier settlers to create conditions and agencies which would facilitate the adjustment of the newcomers to the new environment. Those who came here before 1880, notably the German Jews, though at first considerably disturbed by the avalanche of Jewish immigrants from Russia, Poland and Roumania, soon recalled, directly or indirectly, their own experiences and their own trials and tribulations during their persecutions, thirty or forty years earlier, and quickly responded to the needs of the moment by creating the necessary facilities for meeting the problems which the newcomers faced.

Prior to 1800, Jewish communal activity in New York City and the rest of the United States was largely connected with the synagogue. In 1822, as a result of the request of a Jewish veteran of the Revolutionary War that he be visited in the hospital in New York City where he was confined, the Hebrew Benevolent Society of New York was organized. This society, ostensibly created in order to administer a fund of $300 left after the death of this veteran, later developed into the United Hebrew Charities, now the Jewish Social Service Association of New York City, the largest Jewish organization of its kind in the world. But even before this, stirrings were noticeable in the larger Jewish settlements, particularly in New York City, for the creation of organizations outside of the synagogue for meeting the needs which made themselves felt in the Jewish communities. In New York City, there were at the beginning of the nineteenth century such organizations as a "Female Hebrew Benevolent Society," a "Society for the Education of Orphan Children and the Relief of Indigent Persons," and an agency for the care of unemployed and the prevention of dependency, an agricultural society, and a number of others.

By 1853, The Hebrew Benevolent Society of New York City was aiding 1,200 applicants annually; in 1856 it aided almost 1,900 applicants. On these it spent approximately $5,000 a year. While this may seem a rather small sum today, it should be remembered that there were only between 15,000 and 20,000 Jews in New York City at the time. All of the societies then existing aided between 4,000 and 5,000 persons annually. This, of course, makes the problem of dependency appear as much more serious at that time than it is today. For, even allowing for duplications, it may be conservatively estimated that between 10% and 20% of the Jewish population received assistance from one organization or another. Were this true today, all of the money collected by the Jewish Federation of New York City would not suffice for the needs of this one activity. This was, no doubt, due to the fairly recent immigration of German Jews resulting from the discriminations and persecutions which followed the Napoleonic wars, and continued through the period from 1830 to 1848.

The German Jewish immigrants were no more satisfied with the administration of this organization, which was largely in the hands of the earlier settlers, the Portuguese, than were the Russian immigrants satisfied with the way the Germans conducted their organizations toward the close of the century. In 1844 "The German Hebrew Benevolent Society" was organized, no doubt as a protest against the methods of the Hebrew Benevolent Society. This Society seems to have been very popular. During the first year it had more than 200 members. Sixteen years later (1860) these two organizations combined as a result of public pressure against duplication[52] and formed the United Hebrew Charities.

In 1881 there began the Jewish exodus from Eastern Europe which brought in its wake problems, the magnitude of which challenged the Jewish community of New York and other cities, as never before or since. It seemed to the leaders of the society that the United Hebrew Charities (and the same was true in the other port communities), would be diverted from its original purpose of "distributing relief among needy Hebrews in New York City to the care of Jewish immigrants." At first the organization was alarmed and stated that its function was "to care for the needy of New York City and not of the world." It more or less approved the protective immigration acts of 1882; it sent letters of protest to European leaders and to the press urging more discriminating and more careful selection of immigrants. As the immigration flow continued to increase, the leaders of the Society and indeed of New York Jewry, realized that the time had come for constructive action. They placed an agent at Ellis Island, the port of entry in New York City, to help the immigrants; they opposed the deportation of dependents; they cooperated with the recently formed Union of American Hebrew Congregations, later the Hebrew Immigrant Aid Society for the Care of Immigrants; they established a temporary shelter; and in other ways devised measures and facilities for adjusting the newly arrived immigrants.[53]

The extent of the work of the United Hebrew Charities, which is an indication of the magnitude of the problem faced also in other cities during the years that followed, may be judged from a few figures. In 1882, 300 people received transportation to other cities; in 1883, 1,040 people; in 1892, 4,030 people received transportation with an approximate annual expenditure of $25,000 for railroad fees. In 1882 the total expenditures of the Society were $55,000; in 1883, $90,000. But the work and expenditures continued to mount; more than 600 requests for assistance were received in a single day and more than 8,000 unemployed persons were helped by this organization in 1896. It organized industrial schools for boys and girls; it was largely instrumental in organizing a home for chronic invalids; it was the first to establish a visiting nurses service; it started an experiment for colonizing Jewish immigrants; it established a legal aid society; it organized the Central Russian Refugee Committee in 1890. It became, in a word, the prime mover of various communal activities to assist the residents as well as the newly arrived immigrants.[54]

These activities continued during the twentieth century so that in 1929, before the depression set in, this society spent more than half a million dollars in the care of dependent and maladjusted families. In 1932, it spent approximately a million and a quarter dollars, a substantial share of which came from the general community.

Professionally this organization and other similar organizations throughout the country, developed just as significantly. From a relief society, with the poor coming to the office, standing in line for a mere pittance, it has developed into an organization where families are maintained on a respectable level, are helped to self-support through vocational retraining, through establishment in business, through education and training of their children, and in various other ways. This Society and the other Jewish family societies, have developed standard family budgets and provide their families with a monthly or weekly allowance, carefully calculated to meet their requirements. The attitude of these agencies, their approach and spirit, have developed beyond recognition. They strive as hard as they can to maintain the self-respect of the poor, now known as their "clients." Carefully trained staffs of visitors, usually college and university graduates, and in some cases graduates of professional schools of social work, supervise these families and aim to develop in them constructive forces. Since 1920, when the Jewish Aid Society of Chicago changed its name to the *Jewish Social Service Bureau* of Chicago,[55] most of the larger Jewish agencies in the country, including the United Hebrew Charities of New York City, have similarly changed their names. Instead of Jewish *charities* and Jewish *relief* societies, one now finds Jewish *social service* bureaus or associations in every city with any substantial Jewish population. The change is not merely one of name; it is a change in outlook, point of view, method, and philosophy. Instead of "relief work" we now have "case work," the latter being placed more and more on the basis of fundamental scientific knowledge provided in the social and psychological sciences.

One of the major problems facing these agencies as well as the non-Jewish agencies functioning in this field, is how to utilize, in the case work process, the existing knowledge in the social sciences, and how to develop the necessary knowledge not yet available.[56] It is generally recognized by social scientists that those working with human beings must be equipped not only with the general social sciences but also with an adequate knowledge of the cultural background of the people whom they desire to guide and influence. This is especially true with respect to the Jewish group.[57] What is needed, therefore, is the development of a sociology and social psychology of the Jewish group.[58] Unfortunately, this type of knowledge is not yet in existence.

There is a popular misconception regarding the functions and activities of family agencies. It is commonly believed that they are mainly relief societies whose primary purpose is to provide financial assistance to those who are in need of such aid. Actually, financial relief is only a small although perhaps the most costly aspect of their work. Only between 40% and 50% of the situations dealt with by these agencies require or receive monetary aid. And even these present other problems which require expert treatment because, not infrequently, these problems are the real cause of the financial need. No situation or difficulty is outside their scope.

This was true at least until recently, when some of these agencies changed their policies with respect to the type of situations they would undertake to treat. But it is still true that most of the family agencies will accept almost all problems that human "flesh is heir to." Whether it is conflict between husband and wife, parents and children, children and their schools and other environmental agencies, industrial maladjustment, physical and mental illness, or just plain unanalyzed poverty, the family agency and the family case worker will most likely undertake to render service. In the larger communities there are special agencies for treating some of the more difficult problems requiring special skill or special equipment or both. But the family agency is frequently the hopper which first receives all the problems and difficulties. These are then distributed by it to those agencies which are organized to deal with them.[59]

Some of these developments were in line with those that took place in the non-Jewish agencies. The contribution of the Jewish agencies, however, lies not so much in a different type of work, although that is the case especially in the forms of self-support already mentioned, as in the quality, intensity and standards of work. Jewish agencies in New York, Chicago, Cleveland, Baltimore, and in other cities maintain their families on a very much higher per capita allowance than do the non-Jewish agencies. Before the depression, they were much more discriminating in accepting public relief for their clients than the non-Jewish agencies because of the comparatively low standards of work in the public agencies. They also give greater recognition, implicitly and explicitly, to the differences due to culture, psychological makeup, and inherent potentialities of their clients. In these ways they have made an important contribution to the development of general social work. While the quality of work is uneven among the different societies in the various cities, the better known Jewish societies are among the leaders in their respective cities.

Many of the agencies changed some of their policies and practices during the depression, and are, as a result, much more like the non-Jewish agencies than they were before the depression. This is borne out by figures recently published by the Russell Sage Foundation of New York City, based on information collected by the Foundation from 56 non-Jewish and Jewish family societies throughout the country over a period of more than 11 years. They indicate that such differences as existed between Jewish and non-

Jewish family agencies before the depression, with respect to conditions and standards of work including family allowances and the basis for granting assistance, are rapidly disappearing. The effect of these changes will be discussed in a later connection (See pp. 137–148).

The depression, which began in 1929, and which has continued for seven years, placed an exceedingly heavy burden upon the Jewish family societies, of which there are approximately 100. In 1930, 39 of the largest Jewish family agencies in the country cared for approximately 25,000 Jewish families. In 1931 they took care of about 29,000. In 1932 and 1933 they cared for about 31,000 families. However, in 1934, because of the development of the state and federal relief programs, the load upon Jewish family societies was reduced to about 23,000. This reduction has continued until the current year, when because of a change of policy on the part of the Federal Government, Jewish societies are again called upon to care for larger numbers. But the problem has as yet nowhere reached the proportions of 1932 or 1933.

The expenditures during this period kept pace with the load. Thus in 1929, the 34 largest Jewish family agencies which supplied information spent approximately $2,000,000. In 1930 they spent about $2,130,000; in 1931 about $2,900,000; in 1932 and 1933, about $4,000,000 for each year; in 1934 about $2,390,000; and in 1935, $1,716,000. All of the Jewish family service agencies of which there is record, spent about $4,200,000 in 1935 (See p. 68).

In 1929 and 1930, the same agencies reported a clientele of between 4000 and 4500 families per month requiring financial assistance. In 1931 they aided about 6350 families per month; in 1932 about 9450 families; in 1933, 10,500; in 1934, 6300 families; and in 1935 about 4950. It required about 400 professional social workers to handle this load.[60]

Family Service agencies also care for various types of behavior problems, more especially among boys and girls. These problems are usually treated by the best trained workers. In New York City there is a special organization, the Jewish Board of Guardians, which has a large and especially trained staff for caring for these problems. It also maintains two institutions, one for problem boys and one for problem girls, near New York City. These are the only institutions of their kind maintained by Jews.[61]

In this connection it should be mentioned that there is no reliable information regarding Jewish juvenile and adult delinquency in the United States. Such limited studies as have been made indicate that Jews have less than their numerical proportion of criminals. It is also known that there are important differences in the number and kinds of crimes. Thus, Jews commit very few crimes against the person. Jews also have less than their proportion of juvenile delinquency. There are more delinquents among boys than among girls, and the sentences for girls are much more severe than for boys. But this is due to the greater protectiveness of parents of their daughters. It is only the girl that is absolutely unmanageable who finds her way into court.[62]

What the future of this type of Jewish social work is, nobody knows. It will depend entirely upon the programs of the Federal and State Governments with respect to relief and social security. These programs are at the present time being reconsidered and no one knows what the outcome will be.

B. Health Care

The care of the Jewish sick is in many respects dependent upon the developments in general health care. Methods for treating various types of diseases must be developed in the general field, especially since, with the exception of amaurotic family idiocy and Burger's disease, to which Jews are peculiarly predisposed, and diabetes, which has a greater incidence among Jews than among non-Jews, there seems to be no special Jewish health problem requiring special treatment. Even tuberculosis, which is commonly assumed to be a serious problem among Jews, has in reality a much lower incidence among Jews than in the rest of the white population.[63] However, a number of Jewish hospitals have come to rank among the foremost in the country, and are doing a great deal, not only for the Jewish sick, but for the non-Jewish as well. Although many questions have been raised as to the need or desirability of separate Jewish hospitals, especially since they care for substantial numbers of non-Jewish sick and Jews frequently use non-Jewish hospitals, there is a large body of opinion that Jewish hospitals are essential for the Jewish patient as well as for the Jewish physician. It is fairly well agreed that the Jewish patient is nowhere as comfortable as in a Jewish hospital, whether it be "kosher" or not, and hence is best placed there. Similarly, Jewish physicians and Jewish graduates of medical schools need Jewish hospitals because they find it almost impossible to get interneships and appointments in non-Jewish hospitals. Without hospital facilities the physician is not only helpless in the treatment of disease, but is bound to deteriorate as a practitioner. Inefficient and unethical practices on the part of Jewish physicians react unfavorably not only upon the Jewish patient, but upon the Jewish community as well. It is for these and other reasons that Jewish communities throughout the country have established Jewish hospitals, occasionally jeopardizing the rest of their social service program, because of the heavy drain which hospitals usually are on the community exchequer.

Jewish health care in the United States has in general kept pace with the growth of the Jewish population. The largest Jewish hospital in the United States is admittedly the Mt. Sinai Hospital in New York City, which was dedicated as "The Jews' Hospital" in 1855 and, except for a Jewish hospital in Cincinnati, Ohio, organized in 1850, was the first large Jewish hospital in this country. The progress which Jewish health care has made since the organization of these two hospitals can best be appreciated by a consideration of what the Mt. Sinai Hospital, now one of the largest in the country, was in 1855. Although even at that time it was far removed from the old *Hekdesh*, the traditional ghetto hospital, it was almost as far removed from what the

Mt. Sinai Hospital is today. It had a 150 bed capacity, cost $30,000 to construct, and admitted 271 patients during the first five months. But it had only about 15 to 25 patients at any one time. Its report for 1857 states that its patients consisted of 110 Germans, 64 Polish, 5 native, and 1 Russian Jew. Out of the 285 patients treated during that year, 200 were free. Twenty-eight patients were the largest number at any one time during that year. There was only one resident physician and one salaried surgeon. The salaries of nine paid officials amounted to $1,684, and the total annual expenditure was only $9,700. The hospital owned a burial ground which was probably a convenience and economy! It interested itself in the care of the patients after they left the institution, thereby anticipating present day medical social service.

The expenditure of $9,700 in 1857 should be compared with an expenditure of almost $1,700,000 in 1935, to obtain a proper view of the amazing growth which this hospital has had. The other aspects of its work have had the same kind of development. Thus, for instance, the 285 patients treated in this hospital in that year should be compared with 13,858 patients treated in 1935.[64]

We get something of an idea of the enormous development that has taken place in about eighty years when we realize that today Greater New York alone has 18 hospitals and sanitaria for the care of the Jewish sick, with a capacity of almost 4,000 beds, spending annually about $9,000,000, and that there are close to 70 Jewish hospitals in the United States with a total bed capacity of about 9,000, with an annual expenditure of approximately $19,000,000; that Jewish hospitals throughout the country give a total of more than 2,750,000 days care to the Jewish and non-Jewish sick; also, that there are approximately 4,300 professional persons engaged in these different institutions.[65]

Some of the Jewish hospitals are among the foremost in the country. Hospitals like Mt. Sinai in New York City, Michael Reese in Chicago, Mt. Sinai in Cleveland, Beth Israel in Boston, Jewish Hospital in St. Louis, Cedars of Lebanon in Los Angeles, etc., would be listed among the leading medical institutions in the country. These and the other Jewish hospitals cater not only to the Jewish sick but to the non-Jewish as well. They are centers of research and training for physicians and nurses so that they make their contribution not only to the Jewish but to the general community as well. There are in, addition, between 40 and 50 Jewish clinics and out-patient departments mostly associated with the hospitals. These institutions received 2,295, 793 visits from Jewish and non-Jewish patients during 1935.

The problem of mental disease presents a somewhat different picture. Although it is now well established that Jews have less than their numerically proportionate share of psychoses, the problem of neuroses is fairly serious.[66] Nevertheless, there is not a single hospital, under Jewish auspices, for the care of the mentally ill. They are usually sent to general hospitals for the insane which are maintained by the different states and their subdivisions.

Another problem which has received scant attention in comparison with its importance, is that of chronic disease.

There is only one large private Jewish hospital for chronic diseases in New York City, and none in the rest of the country. Indeed, there are no hospitals for chronic disease in the general community except those maintained by the City, County, or State. These latter are usually run on a rather low level and are little more than poor-farms which receive the broken-down dregs of society. The patient suffering from an incurable ailment may well abandon hope, not only of being cured, but of ending his days in a reasonably decent and satisfactory environment, once he is admitted to such an institution.

The problem is of increasing importance because with the lengthening of the span of life and the intensification of the stresses and strains of modern civilization, more and more people break down only to find that the society which they served and which has developed such excellent facilities for caring for the acutely ill, has made little or no provision for them.

The reasons for this are many and varied. Among the most important are the following: (1) The average stay of patients suffering from acute diseases is about two weeks. The chronically ill require much more extensive care and therefore would reduce the hospitals' turnover were they to be treated in the general hospitals. (2) Chronic diseases are less interesting and less satisfying to the physicians who donate their time and skill to the hospitals. They prefer to treat those diseases and patients that offer the greatest promise for quick cures. They would lose some of their incentive if the general hospitals were to house many chronic patients. (3) Hospital costs and medical fees come very high. The average patient cannot afford a long drawn out illness. Neither the hospital nor the physician can expect the patient to continue to pay for services and treatment over the long periods required by chronic diseases. Since both depend upon fees for their income they necessarily seek to shift the burden to the community. It is because of these and other factors that the private hospital is said to be eager to discharge or transfer patients suffering from chronic diseases to the City hospitals.

The Jewish group faces a special problem in this respect because, as we have seen (p. 5), they are believed to constitute an older group due to the fact that there is so large a proportion of immigrants among them. Moreover, their problems of adjustment as immigrants, their struggle for existence and their stresses and strains because of social and economic discrimination, are probably much more severe than among the rest of the population. It may be expected, therefore, that they will have comparatively large numbers of people who will give way under their burdens. Whether this is so in reality, no one knows. Information regarding Jewish morbidity and mortality is practically non-existent. It is known that the one Jewish hospital for chronic disease has a waiting list of several hundred who are eager to get in, and that many patients find their way to the public institutions to end their days in them.

The Montefiore Hospital for Chronic Diseases in New York City was organized in 1884 in honor of the hundredth birthday of the British Jewish philanthropist, Moses

Montefiore. It was first conceived of as a "Home for Chronic Invalids." If not for the vision and courage of some of its founders and guiding spirits, it no doubt would have remained little more than a glorified infirmary such as may be found attached to most of the larger homes for the aged. It is due to them and their generosity that this hospital is spoken of by the Commissioner of Hospitals of New York City, perhaps the foremost hospital authority in the world, as "a pioneer in the scientific treatment of chronic disease, a leader whose sustained interest commands respect, an institution whose methods are an inspiration and a challenge to all who are charged with the care of the chronic sick."

This hospital has close to 1000 beds of which only about 60 are semi-private with a very nominal charge. The free beds are almost always occupied. With an annual expenditure of more than $1,250,000, only a very small fraction comes from patients; about 40% of its budget comes from the City government and an additional 25% is contributed by the Jewish Federation. Its buildings and grounds represent an investment of over $6,000,000; it has a medical staff of more than 200 physicians some of whom are among the leaders in their respective specialites; it is affiliated with Columbia University for teaching purposes, and carries on an extensive program of research in practically all types of chronic disease. In 1936 it provided about 330,000 hospital days to patients in its city institution and Country Sanatorium for the tuberculous.

One of the most significant aspects of its work is the

manner in which it has been able to overcome the natural handicaps facing an institution for chronic disease. Its major problems in this respect, were the attitudes of the physicians, the patients, and the interest of the community. All of these have been greatly aided by the emphasis on research and the high quality of its work. From a custodial institution it has been converted into a first class hospital or the scientific care of the type of patients who, but a short time ago, were abandoned to their fate. While this hospital has been fortunate in its leaders and sponsors who have made this type of work possible, it may not be too much to hope that other groups, institutions, and communities will follow its lead. There can be little doubt of the need for this type of work.

C. Child Care

The care of Jewish orphans and dependent children in the United States presents a similar picture. From the date when the first Jewish orphans' home in the United States was organized in Charleston, South Carolina, in 1801, this type of Jewish social work experienced great growth and progress. In New York City the first orphan home was opened in 1860, in a rented house which accommodated thirty children. Eight years later, the facilities were enlarged to accommodate 150 children. Today New York City alone has five organizations devoted to the care of dependent children with a total population of 5000 children. There are about 100 organizations throughout the country for the care of dependent children either in institutions or foster homes. They spent, in 1935, almost five and one-half million dollars. Approximately 10,000 Jewish children, of whom only a comparatively small number are full or half orphans, are maintained in these different institutions.

But it is not only in physical facilities for dependent children that enormous progress has been made in the last century. The old conception of child care, from the standpoints of the kind of care to be given, the discipline, the educational facilities, the selection of children, after-care, medical, psychiatric and vocational treatment, etc., has undergone profound changes. Communities now recognize that they have a unique responsibility for the care of the children entrusted to them. Many feel that children so unfortunate as to have been deprived of their parents or to be forced to face life with physical, mental or emotional handicaps, should be given the very best care and attention and such training as will best enable them to compete successfully for a livelihood. The better institutions send their more promising children to colleges and professional schools. Systems of after-care have been organized and every effort is made to help the children overcome their handicaps and to take their places as normal men and women in the communities into which they are discharged.[67]

Two significant developments in child care, departures from the traditional orphans' homes, must be mentioned. One is the cottage plan and the other is the foster home plan. In the first the attempt is made to recreate a family atmosphere for the children through small cottages housing about twenty children of various ages and both sexes, presided over by a "cottage mother" who aims to establish and maintain a spirit and attitude as nearly approximating the normal home as humanly possible. The earliest Jewish cottage home was that of the Hebrew Sheltering Guardian Society in Pleasantville, New York. More modern developments of this same plan are the Jewish child care institutions in San Francisco, Los Angeles, and Cleveland.

A similarly important development is the foster home type of care for dependent children based on the principle that the child develops best in a small family unit. This principle was enunciated at the famous White House Conference of persons interested in child welfare, called by President Theodore Roosevelt in 1909, to consider the best means of caring for dependent and handicapped children. Since that time the tendency has been to place more and more children in small families with foster parents.[68] Theoretically at least the attempt is made to incorporate these children into the family unit and the foster children are supposed to take their places in the homes as do the sons and daughters of the families in which they are placed. The preferences as between institutional and foster care may be gleaned from the fact that whereas the percentage of children in institutions has decreased from 55% in 1929 to 38.7% in 1935, the percentage in foster homes increased from 43.3% in 1929 to 55.4% in 1935. These figures are based on reports of 28 child care agencies.[69]

The controversy as to whether institutional or foster-care is best suited for dependent children has been bitter and acrimonious at times. Each type of care had and still has its strong adherents and opponents. Institutions have been charged with neglecting the emotional side of the child's development; as providing an unnatural environment for children; with inability to care for or to reckon with the individual nature and needs of the child; as poorly equipped to prepare the child for his return to his home or the community; as very expensive because of capital expenditures; etc.

Foster-home care has been criticised as providing poor homes; that foster-parents are interested in the compensation rather than in the children; as requiring frequent transfers and replacements thus imposing an emotional and nervous strain on the children; as unable to provide for joint placements of several children of the same family; as providing little or no opportunity for Jewish education; etc.

Child care workers, agencies, and communities have been striving to develop principles of allocation which would serve as guides for placing children in the type of care best adapted to their needs. Such principles are gradually emerging out of the accumulated experience of the various child care agencies. Some communities established "Clearing Bureaus" for the distribution of children. These bureaus are usually controlled by Boards of Directors composed of representatives of both types of child care to insure adequate consideration of the different interests involved. While these efforts have not always been entirely successful, the conflict and strife are gradually subsiding. Both sides are beginning to realize and admit that each kind of care has a contribution to make and is best adapted to certain types of children.

In a number of communities, Jewish and non-Jewish child-care agencies receive a subsidy from the government for each dependent child. These subsidies amount to hundreds of thousands of dollars annually. In addition to these subsidies dependent children are aided by the State to remain in their own homes by granting a weekly stipend where the father has been removed by death or other causes, through the system of Mothers' Pensions. Not infrequently children are enabled to remain with their relatives, in cases of loss of both parents, through the system of subsidies. In some instances family care societies and child care agencies keep a motherless home intact by placing housekeepers or caretakers in the home.[70]

Neither the cottage plan nor the foster home plan is Jewish in origin. But Jewish agencies have emphasized the notion that the community owes its dependent children the best care possible in order to prepare them to take their place in society. As a result, Jewish child care agencies have developed unusually high standards of work, and in this way have profoundly influenced the general child care field.

Jewish child care did not experience the large fluctuations in the last few years which characterized the work of the family societies. On the whole the years of depression made only a comparatively slight difference in the work of these institutions.

D. Care of the Aged

The care of the Jewish aged is a substantial although not a large problem. There are about 60 old people's homes which care for approximately 6,000 persons.[71] These institutions are maintained from the funds collected by the federations in the different cities. They spend approximately $2,300,000 annually. It is not yet known what the adoption of Old Age Pension provisions in many of the states of the Union will do to this activity. But it is certain that the extent of the problem will not increase.

Among the most important questions troubling homes for the aged the following may be listed: 1. *Admission policies*, such as minimum admission age (usually 60 years); type of investigation and the social, economic and medical criteria to be employed; whether to admit couples; whether to insist on reimbursement from children, relatives, savings and insurance policies, the institution occasionally continuing the premiums and becoming the beneficiary. 2. *Administrative problems*, such as constructive utilization of "inmates' " or "residents' " leisure, frequently solved through occupational therapy, including basketry, weaving, knitting, woodwork, social and recreational activities, etc.; providing opportunity for earning some spending money mainly because of the beneficial effects of such activity and partial independence. 3. *Medical and psychiatric care*, this problem is especially important since almost 50% of the "residents" are chronically ill and physicians do not, as a rule, like such patients for reasons which have been discussed in another connection (See pages 87–91).

CHAPTER VII

ADULT EDUCATION AND RECREATION; YOUTH MOVEMENTS

The recreational problems are dealt with in several ways. There are, first, the activities of the men's and women's clubs connected with synagogues and temples. Then there are various cultural organizations each of which has some type of recreational activity related to Jewish education, broadly conceived. There are, in addition, agencies directly concerned with activities for adult education, such as the Young Men's and Young Women's Hebrew Associations, Educational Alliances, Jewish People's Institutes, Community Centers, etc. There are also Young People's Leagues, devoting at least part of their energies to post-school education. Of all of these activities space will permit only the consideration of the more formal type of organization and its activities, namely, that commonly referred to as the Jewish Center.

The first organization of this type came into existence in 1874 in New York City as the Young Men's Hebrew Association, which is still in existence. Though ostensibly modeled after the Young Men's Christian Association and very largely influenced by the desire on the part of Jewish leaders to keep the Jewish youth from non-Jewish influences by creating similar recreational and educational facilities for them under Jewish auspices, the Jewish Center of today differs in some fundamental respects from its prototypes in the non-Jewish community, the nearest of which are the Young Men's and Young Women's Christian Associations and the social settlements. It differs from the first two in the comprehensiveness of its program, in the non-theological approach to its work, in its efforts to meet the needs of all the members in the community, and in its development of a cultural program. It differs from the settlement in its more democratic form of organization, in the intensive and comprehensive Jewish cultural activities and programs, and in its aim at making its activities self-supporting although few "Centers" have thus far achieved this aim.

Some of the agencies are "community centers" in the broad sense of the term, catering to the needs of young and old, boys and girls, men and women; others limit their activities to only one or more of these groups, such as the Y. M. H. A.'s or the Y. W. H. A.'s, or to a restricted group such as is served by some of the Centers attached to synagogues and temples. But these are in the minority. The majority of these organizations aim to serve all sections of the Jewish population. Some of them have programs of religious, cultural, educational, artistic, vocational, physical education, and general recreational activities. The major problem facing these agencies is the development of programs of recreation and education for character building and self-development on as constructive a basis as possible, which will at the same time be in line with the desires and wishes of their members and clientele who are not always the best judges of what the most valuable programs would be.[72]

The greatest development of Jewish centers in point of numbers took place in the first two decades of the present century. The World War gave a tremendous impetus to these "Centers" by making communities conscious of the need for recreational facilities for their youth. In 1921, the Jewish Welfare Board, organized during the war to serve the Jewish soldiers in the camps in this country and abroad, became the national organization for Jewish Community Centers.

It took over the work previously done by the Council of Young Men's Hebrew and Kindred Associations, and continued to carry on the activities which it had conducted during the World War. It has become the central agency for the development of Jewish Community Centers, Young Men's Hebrew Associations, and similar organizations. It has a membership of more than 300 such organizations, which spend approximately $4,000,000 annually, (See p. 68), and represent an individual membership of about 300,000.

The Jewish Welfare Board developed standards of procedure, principles and policies of operation. It has conducted, for its local agencies, campaigns for buildings, for membership and for maintenance. It publishes *The Jewish Center*, a quarterly, various types of program material, and cooperates with the National Association of Jewish Center Executives. It has continued its interest in the Jewish men in the United States Army and Navy, and also conducts welfare activities for disabled veterans and their families, and for young men in the Civilian Conservation Corps, a recently organized activity by the Federal Government for taking care of the unemployed youth. It has stimulated and supervised the construction of buildings throughout the country. Through publications, field service, and conferences of regional and national scope, it has united these centers into a strong group of organizations serving hundreds of thousands of Jewish youth. It has been estimated that between $30,000,000 and $40,000,000 have been spent by Jewish communities throughout the country in the last two or three decades on buildings to serve the needs of Jewish youth. The Jewish Welfare Board is maintained from the income of an endowment fund created during the War, appropriations from Federations and Welfare funds, (to be discussed later), and donations from private individuals. The "Jewish Centers" are maintained from membership dues, fees, donations of interested individuals, and in some instances by the federations in their local communities.[73]

A number of other organizations are important in this connection. Among these is the B'nai B'rith, which, in its "Wider Scope Activities," carries on a program of education among large numbers of Jews, including college students. These are served by student centers called "Hillel Foundations," with branches on the campuses of about fifteen universities.[74]

Young Judaea, organized in 1909, as a nationalist youth organization, has as its purpose to perpetuate the ideals of Judaism in their relationship to American Jewish life. It aims to unite the Jewish youth and to interest them in the "history of the Jewish people, in a proper understanding of the role of Palestine in Jewish life and in active participa-

tion in its upbuilding as the Jewish National Homeland."
It has about 750 clubs for boys and girls throughout the
country with a membership of approximately 20,000. The
National Organization prepares educational material, suggests programs for the clubs and assists them in the selection
of leaders. It is maintained from individual donations.[75]

The Jewish Chautauqua Society was organized in 1893.
Its activities include publication of textbooks for parents
and teachers, arranging conferences for religious school
teachers in order to develop an interest in Jewish education.
It carries on an educational program by sending rabbis to
summer sessions of the different universities throughout the
United States to lecture on Jewish history, literature, and
culture, before Jewish students and teachers in attendance
during the summer. This organization is maintained by
individual contributions.[76]

There is no such thing as a Jewish youth movement in
the United States, if by that is meant a coordinated, well-
planned and directed activity. There are rather a variety
of organizations each aiming to attract the Jewish youth
to its particular program. The Young Judea, discussed
above, is one of these. There are about 20 other similar
national organizations.

In 1934, when a study of these organizations was undertaken, it was estimated that their combined membership
was between fifty thousand and seventy-five thousand. Of
these 21 organizations, 13 place their emphasis on Zionist
activities. One organization looks upon Palestine as the
means for achieving a program of social justice and universal

brotherhood. Five organizations use Palestine as a means
of adjusting Jewish youth in America to the American environment. Although in general their program is similar to
the 13 organizations mentioned above which have a frankly
Zionist program, they emphasize the American rather than
the Palestine scene. Two organizations aim at the advancement of Judaism.

In general the objectives of youth organizations may be
said to be the following: 1. Rehabilitation of Palestine;
2. Advancement of Judaism; 3. Jewish cultural advancement; 4. Development of social ideals; 5. Jewish unity;
6. Social justice; 7. Combating anti-Semitism.[77]

Curiously, these organizations have not been much concerned with the problem of vocational guidance for American Jewish youth. They have rather been directing their
activities at developing in the youth a Jewish consciousness
and interesting them in Jewish activities. Each of these
organizations is more or less independent of the others, has
its own program, secures funds wherever it can, and is
responsible only to its leaders for what it accomplishes.

CHAPTER VIII

CENTRAL ORGANIZATIONS FOR LOCAL AND NATIONAL NEEDS

A. Central Organizations for Local Purposes

The manifold activities of the Jewish communities already discussed, brought a realization to the leaders of these communities that better organization and coordination are necessary for the most effective work. Toward the close of the nineteenth century the Jewish Federation came into existence, first in Boston in 1895, and in Cincinnati in the following year. At first, these federations and the others which followed, aimed primarily at a more effective collection of funds. Later, especially since the War, and more especially during the third decade of the present century,[78] federations became communal agencies whose function it is not only to provide financial support for their constituent societies but to plan for the community needs along constructive lines. Today, with a few exceptions, the federations aim to support, coordinate, and control the needed social service agencies and activities in their respective communities. Some federations are beginning to shoulder also the burden of raising funds in the local communities for the support of nationwide as well as overseas Jewish activities. Whether directly or through welfare funds, (to be discussed later) national and overseas projects are included in annual drives for funds held in different communities.

There are approximately 70 federations of Jewish charities in the United States today. Practically every community

of any significant size has a federation. They spend about
$10,000,000 annually. In many cities they are the one
central organization which represents all shades of opinion
in the Jewish community. While they are not yet and may
never be the communal organization that one finds in some
communities in Europe, they usually have the support and
good-will of the entire Jewish population.

It should not be inferred from the above that federations are not subject to severe criticism or that all Jews
support the federations in their respective communities.
On the contrary, there is a great deal of criticism of the
philosophy and procedure of federations as we shall see
later (See p. 149 ff). Nor can it be said that federation
support is widespread among the Jewish populations in
the various federation cities. Many federation leaders are
dissatisfied with the extent of community support from
the standpoints of numbers contributing and the amount
of their contributions. Attempts are being made to "widen
the base of contributors."

Table 18 compares the Jewish populations in 28 cities,
the number of contributors to federations and welfare
funds, and the ratio of contributors to the Jewish population. Since these cities have almost 60% of the Jewish
population in the United States and raise almost 75% of
the total amount raised by federations and welfare funds
in the United States, they may be taken as fairly representative, especially since they represent also the different
types of communities with respect to size and community
chest affiliation.

TABLE 18

COMPARISON OF CONTRIBUTORS TO FEDERATIONS AND WELFARE FUNDS
IN 28 CITIES WITH THEIR RESPECTIVE JEWISH POPULATIONS*

Name of City and Type	Estimated Jewish Population	No. Subscribers to Federation and Welfare Funds—1935	Per- cent	Amount Raised
1. *Large Federations*				
Baltimore	68,000	6,735	10.	$ 437,393
Boston	85,000	10,807	13.	505,967
Chicago	350,000	8,630	2.5	1,328,337
New York (Man.-Bronx)	885,000	76,302	8.6	4,047,160
New York (Brooklyn)	797,000	10,714	1.0	449,349
Total	2,185,000	113,188	5.1	$6,768,206
2. *Small and Intermediate Federations*				
Dallas	8,000	1,156	14.	36,761
Montgomery	1,200	279	25.	8,134
San Antonio	6,000	457	75.	15,143
Trenton	11,000	1,174	11.	27,530
York	750	93	13.	1,472
Total	26,950	3,159	11.8	$ 89,040
3. *Welfare Funds*				
Akron	6,500	824	13.	21,382
Ardmore	67	25	37.	648
Canton	4,300	499	12.	9,750
Cincinnati	23,500	2,984	13.	121,575
Cleveland	85,000	6,987	8.	140,540
Columbus	8,500	462	5.	27,359
Detroit	71,268	8,063	11.	444,195
Indianapolis	9,000	1,433	16.	47,421
Lafayette	260	72	28.	3,144
Memphis	10,000	762	0.8	19,429
Minneapolis	22,000	1,551	0.7	33,402
Oakland	6,000	1,164	20.	19,159
St. Louis	50,000	4,191	8.	131,386
San Diego	2,500	216	8.	4,599
San Francisco	38,000	4,429	12.	182,861
Sheboygan	550	56	10.	1,641
Syracuse	14,000	874	6.	11,318
Tyler	500	49	10.	3,000
	351,945	34,641	10.	$1,222,809
GRAND TOTAL	2,563,895	150,988	6.0	$8,080,055

*This table is based, in part, on figures kindly supplied by Messrs. M. Freund and George Wolfe of the Council of Federations and Welfare Funds.

It will be observed from Table 18, that only about 6% of the total Jewish population may be said to contribute to federations and welfare funds. However, this figure is rather misleading, since it is usually the head of the family

who makes the contribution which includes the entire
family. Accordingly, the total Jewish population should
be divided by approximately four (because wealthier families are usually smaller), in order to obtain the number of
families represented. The resultant figure is much more
encouraging. It indicates that out of about 640,000 families
in these cities, 151,000, or about 25%, are represented
among the contributors to federations and welfare funds.
Bearing in mind that according to a study by the Brookings
Institute in Washington, *America's Capacity to Consume*,
for 1929, the most prosperous year in recent history, only
about 35% of the urban families in the United States have
an annual income of $3,000 and over, which might be as-
sumed to be the minimum for voluntary charitable contribution, the number of Jewish contributors seems much
more adequate. This is true unless one assumes that the
Jewish population is differently situated with respect to
income than is the general population. While there may
be some ground for this belief because of the differences in
occupational distribution, there are no data available to
justify such an assumption in the present discussion.

A considerably different and in some ways more dis-
turbing picture of the situation is obtained when the contributions are analyzed. Studies which have been made
indicate that 85% of the funds come from about 14% of the
contributors. What is worse, approximately 54% of the contributions come from about 1¼% of the contributors.[79]
A recent review of the situation by the Joint Distribution
Committee, summarizing its 1936 campaign experience in

47 communities, in which 81,473 contributors gave almost $4,000,000, shows that 1½% of the contributors gave 57% of the funds; 7% gave 23% of the funds; and 91½% of the contributors gave only 20% of the funds.[80]

The large contributors naturally exercise the greatest influence in the federation. Consequently, questions have been raised about the representativeness and democratic nature of federations. These items will be considered later in a critical examination of the Jewish social work situation in the United States. Here, it may be said that the federations and their constituent societies, those which are doing the day by day work in caring for the poor, the sick, the orphans, the widows, the aged, have brought a great deal of credit upon the Jews in this country.

Through the Jewish Federation, Jewish communities have made a contribution of incalculable importance and significance to the general community. The community chests, which serve the general community in the same way as the federations serve the Jewish community, and which are the pride of most of the cities throughout the country, are a direct outcome of the Jewish federations and were profoundly influenced by them. In many instances, the leaders of the general community chests were recruited from among those who were trained in leadership in communal affairs in the Jewish federations. In a number of cities, community chests would have fared badly if the leadership supplied by the Jewish communities had not been available. This is true, not only with respect to personnel but also with respect to the standard of giving. It is well known that Jews give more liberally, proportionately, to their federations as well as to the community chests than do non-Jews. Even today the community chests, in a number of cities, lag behind the Jewish federations in their plan of organization, the adequacy of their allowances to their constituent societies, in the coordination of the work of the societies, and in the responsibility which they feel for the development of organizations to meet new needs in the community.

Having stimulated the creation of the community chest movement, the federations were in turn greatly influenced by it. At first, community chests developed rapidly and made larger funds available to their constituent organizations. Toward the end of the third decade, however, there was a good deal of talk about the "saturation point in giving" having been reached, so that the community chests were much less successful in raising their quotas than formerly. Jewish organizations suffered in common with non-Jewish organizations and they were faced with the dilemma: to remain in the chest and suffer from inadequate financial support, falling behind in the progressive march which characterized some of the non-chest federations; or to withdraw from the community chest, be charged with separatism, disloyalty, etc., but have the opportunity of developing their work as did the other cities. They chose to remain in the chests and sought other ways of meeting their special needs.

There are a number of problems which Jewish federations in community chests must face sooner or later. Some of these have already presented themselves in one way or another in the different communities. It is to be regretted that no one has thus far studied these problems in all their ramifications and implications. No one can say, therefore, that community chest affiliation is good or bad for the Jewish communities; that they should be continued, modified, or abandoned. No authoritative statement along these lines will be possible until the relationships will be thoroughly studied and conclusions drawn from an objective examination of the experiences to date. Partisan statements and arguments, for or against, have but little value other than to indicate the areas and type of questions to be studied.

Among the more important questions which should be considered in this connection the following may be listed:

1. What is the effect of community chest affiliation on anti-Semitism, either existing or potential? It is sometimes argued that such affiliation tends to refute the charge of Jewish separatism and clanishness, makes for better understanding between Jews and non-Jews, provides for more intimate contacts, gives each group insight into the other's problems, etc. On the other hand, it has been suggested that the differences in standards and requirements of Jewish agencies and individuals, which are not infrequently higher than the non-Jewish, are likely to cause friction, irritation, and possibly ill feeling. This because the funds coming from the same source should presumably be distributed on the same basis and in accordance with the same standards.

Some communities have already faced this problem and

it was not easy to explain to those in charge of the distribution of community chest funds, why Jewish families should have more liberal allowances than the non-Jewish families when the funds are derived from the entire community. The dangers of misunderstanding in such a procedure are obvious. It has been suggested, also, that one way of solving this problem would be for the Jewish community to raise supplementary funds for this purpose. But this, too, is open to misinterpretation. Some community chest leaders may assume that all available funds for local relief purposes should be given to the chest and that any funds collected by the Jewish community for supplementary purposes would have gone to the chest if there were no need for additional funds for local Jewish needs.

2. Another problem along the same lines arises from the possibility of the Jewish community receiving more from the chest than Jewish contributors give to it. In a sense this is a contradiction of the fundamental philosophy and principles of the community chest. For affiliation with the chest on the part of the Jewish or any other group should not be on a *quid pro quo* basis. Ideally every member of the community should give as much as he can afford. Others should receive as much as they need or the chest can afford. No one is supposed to know how much a given group gives or receives from the chest. In reality, however, the situation is quite different. Since the Jewish group has membership in the receiving-end of the chest through its social agencies or through the Jewish federation,

it is not difficult to determine how much these agencies receive from it. And, although it is more difficult to determine how much is contributed by Jews, this is not impossible of accomplishment. Some people have had the feeling that subversive of the best principles of the community chest as such figures and comparisons are, they have been resorted to.

Jewish community leaders, especially those who are also leaders in the chest, are frequently uneasy about the matter. They realize only too well that such calculations are not only unfair but are likely to be injurious to the Jewish position in the community. They are no less dangerous for the community integration which should flow from community chest participation. The unfairness derives from the fact that in such calculations no allowance is made for the non-Jewish work which Jewish agencies such as hospitals and settlements are doing. All of it is likely to be charged as going to Jews. On the other hand Jews are bound to receive less credit than is their due at the contributions end. First because not all Jewish contributors may be known as Jews; and second because contributions from large corporations where Jews are stockholders are never credited to Jews even though the contributions are ultimately paid for by the stockholders. It will be clear, therefore, that in any such comparisons, Jews would be debited with more than they receive and credited with less than they give. However this does not mean that the comparisons, unfair as they may be, may not be made. The awareness of the possibility is frequently a source of concern to the Jewish leaders with the result that they over-compensate at both ends; bringing pressure upon Jewish contributors for more generous contributions; and using their influence with the Jewish agencies for moderate budgetary requests.

3. A third problem relates to the effect which community chest affiliation has upon Jewish leadership. One of the arguments in favor of community chest affiliation is the opportunity which it gives Jewish leaders for activity in and contributions to broader fields. But these opportunities are not always an unmixed blessing so far as the Jewish community is concerned. They not infrequently result in diffusion of interest, dissipation of energy, and divided loyalty.

4. A similar problem is the influence upon Jewish contributors. As already indicated, Jewish standards of giving and receiving are higher, proportionally, than the non-Jewish. In the beginning it was hoped that Jewish standards would influence the non-Jewish standards. But experience proved otherwise. Whether it is because of the difference in campaign methods, indirectness of claim and appeal, or the lower standard of contributions among non-Jews, it is generally assumed that Jewish contributions to the chest are on a lower level than are their contributions to distinctly Jewish causes. Nevertheless, their contributions to the chest are almost invariably more generous, in proportion to their wealth, than are the non-Jewish contributions.

5. The effect of community chests on the Jewish agencies can be surmised from the foregoing. But the struggles for

higher standards, even though they may be defeated at times, are by no means the greatest disadvantage they face. Much more serious is the feeling, not infrequently expressed, that since the financial support comes from the same source and since the standards are or should be more or less the same, there is little justification for maintaining separate Jewish agencies. Proposals are occasionally made for merging Jewish with non-Jewish agencies in order to save administrative expenses; or to place Jewish workers in non-Jewish agencies to handle Jewish problems. Although such instances are still relatively few they come with greater frequency and greater insistence. Similarly, it is much more difficult to create new organizations for meeting new needs when the funds must be obtained from the chest than from the federation. This is not so much because it is more difficult to get appropriations from the chest than from the federation, as it is due to the greater reluctance on the part of the Jewish leaders to seek the funds from the chest.

6. In addition to the foregoing there is some question whether chest support of Jewish agencies does not tend to weaken Jewish interest in and identification with the Jewish agencies and problems.

It has been pretty well established that the process of fund raising for community needs is one of the best means of educating the community to an intelligent appreciation of its needs and problems as well as some of the factors giving rise to them. Where the fund raising is done for the entire community there is less opportunity for emphasizing the specifically Jewish needs and problems. This is bound to result in a lessening of the sense of responsibility on the part of the Jews for Jewish needs. Although this has been offset in some degree by the welfare-fund movement which, as we shall see presently, raises funds for specifically Jewish causes, the problem nevertheless exists. It has become aggravated during the depression years by governmental assumption of the responsibility for some of the activities formerly carried by private agencies.

Despite these and other limitations of the community chests there can be little doubt that they have been of great benefit to Jewish agencies at least during the depression. They have provided resources and stability which might otherwise not have been available during one of the most difficult periods of American history. It is estimated that in 1935 Jewish agencies in 63 cities, having a total annual expenditure of approximately $7,100,000, received $4,077,000, or about 43% of their funds from community chests. The extent of Jewish affiliation with community chests may be judged from the fact that out of 140 cities having chests, 83, or almost 60%, include the Jewish agencies. Out of 80 cities having Jewish federations and community chests, 52, or 65% of the federations, are in the chests.[81]

In the last decade or so there has developed in the United States a central financial organization, commonly known as the "Welfare Fund," for the purpose of supporting non-local philanthropic services, such as the national and overseas agencies. The creation of the "Welfare Fund" was due in part to the fact that the federations were handicapped in their support of non-local activities because contributors occasionally insisted that their contributions were designed to assist local agencies. A more important factor, however, was the fact that many federations were affiliated with general community chests which are of a strictly local character. It was impossible for these community chests to support Jewish agencies whose activities were cultural or were outside the particular city. A means had to be found for enabling the Jewish community to collect funds for the support of those organizations, whether local or non-local in character, which could not be included in the community chest set-up.

At the present time there are about 30 welfare funds in the country. There are as yet no generally acceptable criteria for judging either the need for or quality of work of a given national or overseas agency or its eligibility to welfare fund support. The tendency, however, is in the direction of creating the necessary standards.

In the last few years the dissatisfaction with the representativeness of federations and welfare funds expressed itself in the demand for a more representative organization. Several communities have been experimenting with a "Community Council," which is made up of representatives from all the organizations interested in communal problems and activities. It is altogether too early to attempt to evaluate this experiment. In Cleveland, Ohio, where a Council was organized about two years ago, those who have been close to the work seem pleased with its achievements thus far, especially since it has been able to make some headway and achieve some success with difficult community problems, as for example, the aggravated problem of *Kashrut* (Kosher meat).[82] But young as is this experiment, it is not without some critics. There are some who see in it another instrument for controlling community activity by the same people who now control the federations and welfare funds.[83] Others see in such criticism a poorly veiled attempt on the part of the critics to seize control of this activity for their own purposes. To the non-partisan observer it seems to represent an interesting effort at democratizing American Jewish community organization.

B. National Agencies

The national organizations referred to in the preceding paragraphs in connection with welfare funds, constitute a large portion of Jewish communal work in this country. It is difficult to say how many such organizations there are, but it may be safely estimated that between 40 and 50 national organizations, spending about five and one-half million dollars annually, are partly supported by federations and welfare funds. A national organization may be defined roughly as an agency which serves no particular locality but the country as a whole. It may do its work in the United States or overseas, or both at home and abroad.

National agencies, for our present purposes, may be grouped under six headings. There are, first, the medical agencies. These are hospitals located mainly in Denver, Colorado, and Los Angeles, California, for the care of tuberculous patients either while the disease is active or quiescent. Some of these agencies also care for the families of the patients. There are five such agencies spending approximately one million dollars annually.

A second group of national agencies may be said to consist of agencies doing educational and cultural work. Among these might be mentioned The B'nai B'rith in its "wider scope" activities; The Jewish Chautauqua Society; The National Farm School; The Jewish Publication Society; Young Judaea; The Menorah Association; etc.

A third group of national organizations includes the civic and protective agencies: The American Jewish Committee; The American Jewish Congress; The Anti-Defamation League of the B'nai B'rith; The Jewish Labor Committee; and the Jewish Telegraphic Agency. This agency is included among the organizations functioning for the protection of civic rights because without some such service as that rendered by it the work of the others would be seriously hampered. Its form of organization was changed recently from a private enterprise operated for profit to a communally owned agency with a responsible Board of Directors which determines its policies. This group expends approximately $500,000 per year.

The fourth group consists of a number of agencies concerned with community service and coordination. Among these may be mentioned: The National Conference of Jewish Social Service; The Graduate School for Jewish Social Work; The National Desertion Bureau, which though located in New York serves also other communities; The Jewish Welfare Board, already discussed in connection with adult education (p. 99); The Council of Jewish Federations and Welfare Funds; The National Coordinating Committee for Aid to German Refugees; The German Jewish Children's Aid, Inc.; etc.

A fifth group may be said to consist of such agencies as the Conference on Jewish Relations; Hebrew Immigrant Aid Society, primarily concerned with aiding immigrants and their relatives; The National Council of Jewish Women, which is also concerned with immigrants, especially immigrant girls and women. It also does other types of work including granting assistance to poor students in obtaining an education, either through its own funds or through its auxiliary, the Council of Jewish Juniors, an organization of Jewish young women; etc.

The sixth group consists of agencies for overseas reconstruction and relief. Among these should be mentioned: The Joint Distribution Committee; The ORT; The American Palestine Campaign; The Jewish National Fund; The Hadassah; The American Friends of the Hebrew University; etc.

Space does not permit detailing the work of these agencies. Nevertheless a few should be briefly described in addition to those already discussed.[84]

Among the most important national agencies from the standpoint of social work is the National Conference of Jewish Social Service (recently changed to "Welfare"). As organized in 1899, it was composed of lay and professional persons. More recently, it has developed its activities along distinctly professional lines. In the last decade and a half, its annual meetings have been devoted to the development of a professionally conscious and technically trained group of men and women devoting themselves to professional problems. This Conference was directly or indirectly responsible for the establishment of several organizations of national scope, most important of which are the National Desertion Bureau, an organization already mentioned, which devotes itself to locating the husbands of deserted wives; and The Graduate School for Jewish Social Work. It has published proceedings of its annual meetings since 1900 and issues a quarterly journal, *The Jewish Social Service Quarterly*.[85]

In the Graduate School for Jewish Social Work, organized in 1925, a facility was created for training young men and women to engage in Jewish social work as a profession. This School is a national institution, strictly graduate in character requiring the Bachelor's degree for admission, with a faculty consisting of some of the foremost Jewish social workers and scholars in the country. It is authorized by the Regents of the State of New York to give the Master's and Doctor's degrees. The course of study is two years. It has drawn its students from, and distributed them to, all parts of the country. In the twelve years of its existence it has had an enrollment of about 1000 persons who have taken either part or the full course of study. It has undertaken various types of research on the different aspects of Jewish life in America.[86] It has maintained its work on a level equal to the best general schools of social work. Since 1928 it has been a member of the American Association of

Schools of Social Work, comprising more than 30 general schools of social work connected with American universities, and its Director was President of the Association for two years, (1932–1934). In this way it has materially influenced social work education in the United States.[87]

Another important national agency from the standpoint of Jewish social work is the Bureau of Jewish Social Research. This organization, created in 1919, has conducted surveys of Jewish communal activities in most of the communities in the country. In this way it was instrumental in affecting the standards and activities of most of the Jewish social agencies. In 1935 it was merged with the newly-created National Council of Federations and Welfare Funds. This latter organization, (the word "National" in its name was dropped in 1936), aims to coordinate the work of the federations and welfare funds . It continues the field service by the "Bureau," formerly conducted for the purpose of stimulating a wider participation of lay leadership in Jewish social work. It has annual and regional meetings for the purpose of considering current problems and recent trends and tendencies. Most of the federations and welfare funds are constituents of this organization. It publishes *Notes and News*, periodically, and, in 1935 and 1936, issued *the Jewish Social Work Year Book* for 1934 and 1935 respectively.

About three years ago there was organized in New York City, The Conference on Jewish Relations. Its purpose is to inquire into the social, educational, and economic problems of Jewish adjustment in America. This organization is still in the formative stage and it cannot yet be said what its program or future will be. Thus far it has emphasized activities which throw light on problems of economic adjustment and anti-Semitism. It aims to be scientific in its approach by undertaking and encouraging others to undertake studies and publications in the fields of its interests. Recently, (June 1937), it announced the publication of a scientific quarterly journal, *Jewish Social Studies*, with the first issue scheduled to appear in the Fall of 1938. It has maintained itself and its program through membership dues, contributions from interested individuals, and the devoted services of a few of its leaders.[88] Its membership consists very largely of professional men and women.

The National Coordinating Committee for Aid to German Refugees was organized in 1934, through the efforts of James G. McDonald, High Commissioner for Refugees from Germany, of the League of Nations. The activities of this organization are national and overseas in scope. It acts as a central registry and clearing bureau for all organizations interested in the refugee problem; refers to appropriate agencies cases of immigrants needing assistance; handles special problems for which no other agency is prepared to assume responsibility; organizes local committees for distributing refugees in the interior cities; explores possibilities for employment throughout the United States; deals with special immigration and deportation cases; cooperates with Federal and State labor departments on questions of passports and immigration procedure; subsidizes the transportation and other expenses for repatriation; secures information from abroad for those who have relatives there; etc.

The German-Jewish Children's Aid, Inc., chartered under the laws of the State of New York in 1934, has undertaken the education and placement of 250 German-Jewish children brought to the United States. Two hundred and thirty-six children have already arrived and are being cared for at the present time in private families in 58 cities in 19 states, under the supervision of professionally equipped child welfare agencies.

CHAPTER IX

PARTICIPATION IN JEWISH EFFORTS IN OTHER COUNTRIES

A. For Relief and Reconstruction

Among the national organizations engaged in relief and reconstruction in other countries, the largest and most important is the American Jewish Joint Distribution Committee, or as it is usually referred to, The Joint Distribution Committee, or J.D.C. This organization was established in 1914, through the efforts of three organizations which were engaged in collecting funds to relieve the suffering Jewish victims of the World War.[89] The J.D.C. has operated in more than 40 countries and has disbursed approximately $84,000,000. The largest sums were expended in behalf of the Jews of Poland, Russia, and Palestine. Prior to 1921, the J.D.C. extended emergency aid. Since 1921, the Committee's program has been largely devoted to economic and social rehabilitation. In the Soviet Union the J.D.C. developed a large land settlement program, strengthened and supported Jewish mutual aid societies, loan kassas, medical associations, workshops and courses for trade training. In Palestine, it organized the Malaria Research Unit, established the Palestine War Orphans Committee, supported the Loan Bank, Ltd., organized the Central Bank of Cooperative Institutions, contributed to the Hebrew University, and turned over substantial sums to the Palestine Economic Corporation. The J.D.C. established the following per-

manent organizations for economic aid: the American Joint
Reconstruction Foundation, which has promoted Jewish
credit loan work throughout Eastern and Central Europe;
the Agro-Joint (American Jewish Joint Agricultural Corporation), which has initiated and directed land settlement
and industrial training activities in the Soviet Union; and
the Palestine Economic Corporation, which has developed
commercial, industrial, and agricultural undertakings and
a large housing program in Palestine. Since the Hitler
regime in Germany, the J.D.C. helped the Jewish leaders
of that country organize a Central Committee for Relief and
Reconstruction, and has subventioned and collaborated
with that organization. The J.D.C. likewise participated
in the establishment of the High Commission for German
Refugees, and has granted substantial sums to refugee aid
organizations. It has also cooperated with the Jewish Colonization Association, with the Central British Fund for
German Jewry, with HICEM (an organization directing
Jewish immigration), and with the major refugee aid committees all over the world. During the years 1933, '34, '35,
the J.D.C. made appropriations for its programs abroad
totalling $2,830,000. The J.D.C. receives its income from
various local campaigns, Welfare Funds, and federation
drives. Those who are acquainted with the work and achievements of this organization view it, despite such criticisms
as may be made of various phases of its work, as the greatest single effort on the part of the Jewish people of one
country for the welfare of the Jews of other countries,
recorded in Jewish history.[90]

Closely associated with the Joint Distribution Committee from the standpoint of interested personnel though independent in every other way, are two organizations especially designed to meet the needs of German refugees: The Refugee Economic Corporation and the Emigrè Charitable Fund, Inc. These organizations aim to deal with the situation created by the Nazis as a result of the measures they took against religious and political minorities which deprived large numbers of the means of earning a livelihood and forced them to flee, frequently for their very lives. It became clear that relief alone was insufficient, especially since most countries, because of their own unemployed, sought to prevent competition by foreign labor. To meet the needs for new outlets, the Refugee Economic Corporation and the Emigrè Charitable Fund, Inc. investigate and finance economic opportunities throughout the world. The Refugee Economic Corporation, (R.E.C.) is a stock company seeking to make its investments so as to safeguard its principal, wherever possible, while creating employment and other opportunities for refugees. The Emigrè Charitable Fund, on the other hand, is ready to undertake expenditures without expectation of repayment. The two organizations have provided a number of loan funds in foreign countries with which independent enterprises are financed thus enabling refugees to make a fresh start. Large colonization projects are also being developed and financed by these funds.

Another organization also functioning overseas is the ORT (abbrev. for the Russian name:—*Obshtchesvo*

Rasprostranenia Truda and the French:—*Organisation de Reconstruction du Travail*), founded in 1880. At the close of the World War, ORT began its work in Poland, Roumania, Latvia, Lithuania, and Russia. The program of the ORT is to promote and support trade and vocational education among the Jewish masses in Eastern and Central Europe; to maintain and encourage Jewish agricultural activities in the Soviet Union, Poland, Roumania, Latvia and Lithuania; to assist individual artisans in cooperative enterprises and raise the general level of Jewish work and handicraft. Since the Hitler regime it established a vocational school in Paris and an agricultural colony in the South of France, and is training young German men and women in an agricultural colony and in trade schools in Lithuania. The ORT has from time to time conducted its own campaigns for funds. In the main, however, it has secured its funds through special arrangements with J.D.C. It is also a beneficiary of federation and welfare fund drives.[91]

There are a number of other organizations functioning abroad, such as the Federation of Polish Jews, aiming to aid the Jews in Poland; a similar organization for Roumania; and several organizations that are interested in promoting Jewish settlement in Biro-Bidjan, the area in the far-East, set aside by the Soviet government, in which a Jewish autonomous republic is to be developed.

B. Activities for Palestine

There are many organizations in the United States whose activities are exclusively directed to collecting funds and

conducting educational work for Palestine. Little more can
be done here than to enumerate the most important of them
and to indicate briefly their nature and extent.

The most important is probably the Zionist Organization of America, which carries on a program of education
and propaganda on behalf of Palestine. It has branches in
most of the cities in the United States and a number of subsidiary organizations, all engaged in work for Palestine.
Another organization, the American Palestine Campaign,
created in 1931, now the United Palestine Appeal, is the
fund-raising instrument in the United States for the Jewish
Agency for Palestine, (*The Keren Hayesod*), the Jewish
National Fund, (*Keren Kayemeth*), and the Central Bureau
for the Settlement of German Jews in Palestine. The United
Palestine Appeal is the successor to a series of fund-raising
efforts for Palestine in the United States extending back
to 1919.[92]

A third organization is the Jewish National Fund of
America, which collects funds for the purchase of land in
Palestine. It is estimated that up to October 1, 1935, it
raised approximately $5,000,000 for this purpose.[93] A fourth
important organization is Hadassah, the Women's Zionist
Organization of America. This organization, created in
1912, has almost 500 senior and junior chapters in 274
cities in the country, with a total membership of 45,000.
It has thus far engaged primarily in health work in Palestine, its activities including the maintenance in Palestine of
hospitals, clinics, research, medical social service, instruction in dietetics in schools, school hygiene, playgrounds,

etc. It also conducts an active educational campaign in this country through publications and a speakers bureau for the purpose of interesting Jewish women in Palestine. Recently it undertook the task of building the University Hospital and Post-Graduate Medical School of the Hebrew University in Palestine, in conjunction with the American Jewish Physicians Committee.[94]

There are a number of other organizations for Palestine, such as the Palestine Economic Corporation, the American Economic Committee for Palestine, American Friends of the Hebrew University, the National Labor Committee for the Jewish Workers in Palestine, the Mizrachi Palestine Fund, the New Zionist Organization (Revisionists), The Jewish State Party, The League for Labor Palestine, Pioneer Women's Organization, and many affiliated youth organizations.

While there is no way of determining exactly how much the overseas agencies collect, it may be safely said that on the average about $4,000,000 a year are contributed by American Jewry for purposes of overseas work. In the current year (1937) the J.D.C. and the United Palestine Campaign are each campaigning for about $4,500,000. In 1936, they each campaigned for about $3,500,000 but neither organization reached its goal. In 1934 and 1935 these two organizations conducted a united campaign. If they are successful in raising the $9,000,000 this year, it will be the largest sum American Jewry ever contributed for overeas work during one year. Since both organizations get a large portion of their funds from federations and welfare funds, it was necessary to arrive at some arrangement for avoiding the competition and rivalry for appropriations which developed in the campaigns of 1936. Accordingly, an agreement was reached whereby the Joint Distribution Committee is to receive 60% of the funds raised for overseas work and the United Palestine Campaign, (comprising the American Palestine Fund, the Jewish National Fund, The Mizrachi Organization and the Zionist Organization of America) is to receive 40%. This agreement applies only to those cities where a welfare fund or a federation conducts the campaign.

CHAPTER X

OTHER ORGANIZATIONS AND ACTIVITIES

1. *Social.*—In addition to the organizations and activities outlined in the foregoing pages, there are a great many which are not usually included among social service agencies but which are, nevertheless, important for the cultural life and social organization of the Jewish people in the United States. A complete picture of organized Jewish life in this country would have to include the less formal organizations for social, cultural and perhaps even political activity.

In the first group of organizations,—those organized for social purposes,—might be mentioned the many unaffiliated organizations frequently referred to as "ladies societies," but not always limited to women, who carry on philanthropic activities. There are many such organizations in each Jewish community. They not infrequently interfere with the community-wide organizations, but many enlightened professional social workers have worked with them and have secured their cooperation for the advantage of all concerned.[95]

The lodges and fraternal organizations are mainly organized for mutual aid purposes. While it is not known how many such organizations there are and how many members they have, eleven of the largest organizations report a total membership of more than 330,000.[96] These and many other similar organizations perform educational, recreational and insurance functions. In many instances they pay sick and death benefit, maintain institutions to provide for the health and recreation of their members, have a socialized type of medical assistance, maintain burial grounds, etc.

Hundreds of thousands of foreign born Jews belong to *Landsmanschaften*, societies organized and named in accordance with the place of birth or old-world residence of the members. The number of these societies, which are found in all cities with a large Jewish population, is not known, although it is estimated that there are several thousand of them. Many of the individual societies are in turn members of one of the several central *Landsmanschaften* which were organized mainly for the purpose of rendering assistance to the respective Jewish communities abroad. The last decade and a half saw a diminution in the extent and activities of these societies. But the increasing Jewish misery abroad in recent years has given them a new lease on life. They are now very actively engaged in all types of relief work and diplomatic intervention. The Federation of Polish Jews, a central organization of Polish *Landsmanschaften*, is conducting its own campaign for funds for the relief of the Jews in Poland. The Roumanian Jews have a similar organization with similar activities, and a Federation of Galician Jews was organized as late as January, 1937. Most individual *Landsmanschaften* run joint campaigns with the respective branches of fraternal orders for the relief of the Jews in their native towns and cities. The extent of their activities and collected funds are unknown. The *Landsmanschaften*, the local branches of fraternal orders,

and smaller American relief societies, are now being drawn
into local American-Jewish community activities. Many
of them participate in the community councils. A great
many are active in the Jewish federations of charities and
in the various protective organizations.

An interesting type of organization is the "family society,"
composed of members of a given family and their relatives
through marriage. There is no information as to how many
there are, or what are their activities and programs. But
it is known that there are a great many of them. They
carry on many social, mutual aid, and philanthropic activities. The larger of them provide the same advantages as
the lodges and fraternal organizations.[97]

A peculiarly American organization is the National Greek
Letter Fraternity of college students and alumni. It began as
an attempt to meet the need created by the discrimination
against Jewish students by the general fraternities and
sororities. It is estimated that there are almost 63,000
members in 29 such national Jewish fraternities.[98]

2. *Cultural.*—Among the organizations for cultural activities must be mentioned the libraries, publication societies,
academic societies, theatres, the Yiddish and English-Jewish
press, etc.

There are nine outstanding libraries largely devoted to
the collection of Jewish books, periodicals, manuscripts and
ceremonial objects. The leading library is that of the Jewish
Theological Seminary of America, which has the largest
collection of Jewish books and ceremonial objects in the

world. The library of the Hebrew Union College, in Cincinnati, is the second largest. Other important collections worthy of mention are those of the Rabbi Isaac Elchanan Theological Seminary and Yeshiva College in New York City; The American Jewish Historical Society and The Jewish Institute of Religion both in New York City; The Hebrew Theological College in Chicago; The Dropsie College in Philadelphia; The Graduate School for Jewish Social Work in New York; and the recently organized Central Jewish Library and Archives in New York. Mention should also be made of the Jewish collections maintained by the Jewish Division of the New York Public Library, Columbia, Harvard, and Yale Universities.

Scholarly activities in the Jewish field are conducted, and their results published, by a number of organizations. Among those worthy of mention are: the American Academy for Jewish Research; The American Jewish Historical Society; The Jewish Academy of Arts and Science; The American Section of the Yiddish Scientific Institute; the faculties of several universities, such as Columbia and Harvard; Seminaries, schools, and Rabbinical associations. The Jewish Publication Society of America has published a large number of volumes on various aspects of Jewish life. Its collection constitutes the most important contribution to Jewish literature made by a single organization in this country. There are also several other publication agencies, but none can compare with the Jewish Publication Society.

The Yiddish and English-Jewish press represents an important influence in Jewish cultural life. There are five Yiddish daily newspapers, about twenty periodicals, and ten or more periodicals using both English and Yiddish. It is estimated, that there are more than 100 English-Jewish periodicals. There are also about ten Hebrew periodicals and one Ladino weekly. The Yiddish theatres, too, are very important in this respect. A recent study (1933)[99] of the Yiddish theatre in New York City showed that the season opened with nine Yiddish theatres in New York City but five were forced to close before the season was over. The Yiddish Art Theatre was the best known among them. Many of its performances such as "The Dibbuk," "Yoshe Kalb," "Green Fields," etc., were seen by many non-Jews and were highly praised by the dramatic critics in the general press. It would seem, however, that the Yiddish theatre is not as prosperous today as it was a few years ago. During its heyday it contributed a number of very fine artists to the English stage.

3. *Political.*—There are practically no Jewish organizations for political purposes. Various attempts have been made from time to time to organize Jewish groups for political activity but these have been repudiated by the Jewish community and have, therefore, never made any real headway. During election campaigns, the political parties, in their efforts at obtaining votes, create Jewish organizations to sponsor their respective candidates, and individual candidates occasionally raise Jewish issues. But it is not long before the Jewish and general public become aware of the

motivations and they are repudiated. The Presidential campaign of 1936 is a case in point. The major political parties, such as the Democrats and Republicans, maintain no Jewish organizations except during campaign periods, when they create special speakers' and information bureaus. The radical parties, such as the socialists and communists, do maintain Jewish sections which are more or less active all the time.

CHAPTER XI

PRESENT TRENDS IN JEWISH SOCIAL
WORK IN THE UNITED STATES

The foregoing survey would be incomplete without a critical analysis of the present trends and tendencies in Jewish social work. While in general they are similar to the trends in general social work, there are some special problems which must be borne in mind in order fully to appreciate the existing situation.

Before embarking upon this analysis it seems necessary to caution the reader that since this is to be a critical analysis of the trends and tendencies, all of which implies interpretation, it may no longer be possible to be strictly objective. Something of the writer's point of view must necessarily find its way into the interpretation. However, the aim will be to reduce this to a minimum.

A. The Depression and Its Influence

Until 1929, and especially since the World War, Jewish social work made enormous progress, qualitatively and quantitatively. It is safe to say that never before in Jewish history, either in this country or elsewhere, has comparable progress been made in Jewish community organization in a like period. It seemed, indeed, as if a golden age were to be inaugurated in this respect, for the Jewish communities in this country. Then came the depression. It brought a serious challenge to Jewish social work. At first it seemed as if Jewish social work were destined for unprecedented expansion because of the depression. As the needs became manifest greater funds were made available for meeting them. Gradually, as the funds from Jewish sources became more limited, additional and larger sums were secured first through non-sectarian drives and later through governmental subsidy. Expenditures grew by leaps and bounds. Staffs were increased to meet the avalanche of new cases. But Jewish agencies could no more meet the needs with a trained personnel and adequate work than could the non-Jewish agencies. Standards were lowered; untrained people were taken on so that in many instances they outnumbered the trained and experienced people; superficial work became the rule. Discouragement followed in the wake of these conditions.

Several other factors due to the depression must be mentioned here for they may be important influences in determining the future of Jewish social work in this country. These are: first, the developing public social work program; second, the changed attitude of Jewish social workers toward Jewish social work; and third, the economic philosophy of some of the younger Jewish social workers.

The deepening depression made it clear that private philanthropy was unequal to the problem which the increasing unemployment brought in its wake. Many felt that even if private philanthropy were able to deal with the problem, victims of the depression who are able and willing to work but can find none through no fault of their own, should not be forced to apply to charity but should be aided by the government whose duty it is to care for its citizens. Jewish social workers were among the first to express themselves on this score in unmistakable terms at a time when the federal government was most reluctant to recognize that it had any responsibility along those lines.[100]

Gradually municipalities developed means and set aside funds for caring for the unemployed. The soundness and logic of this development, the inadequate funds available to Jewish agencies from Jewish sources, the inherent dislike that most people have for becoming dependent on private charity, and a constantly diminishing income on the part of federations and community chests, made it inevitable that Jewish agencies should welcome this development. Many of them turned over large numbers of their clients to the public agencies, irrespective of the type of care they would receive. In some communities the Jewish agencies were enabled, through a system of compensation and subvention from public funds, to continue to care for their Jewish clients. But this did not always prove to be a satisfactory arrangement, for it meant increases in numbers of clients and staff beyond the agencies' absorptive capacity. It played havoc with existing standards.

Whether Jewish agencies kept their clients at first, when the federal government subsidized some private agencies, and turned them over after the federal government decided, in 1933, to work only through public agencies, or whether they turned them over to the public agencies as soon as they were created, it soon became clear that the Jewish agencies carried but a small portion of their problem. It became equally clear that without the aid of the public agencies the Jewish organizations could have carried the burden only with great difficulty.[101]

While, with some, the departure from traditional practice of the Jewish community caring for its dependent population raised questions about the wisdom and desirability of this practice, it seemed to fit in well with the aims and desires of others in the Jewish communities. The contributors saw in it a desirable release from burdens which they were unwilling or unable to carry. Some Jewish culturists, who had been finding fault with the Jewish community for spending so much of its substance on the old, the sick, the poor, in a word, the so-called "abnormal" members of the community, saw an opportunity for diverting the funds used for relief to cultural activities. The former, they argued, should be paid for by the state; Jewish funds should be used for "constructive" purposes.[102] They did not realize that the Jewish people, or at least the contributing portion of it, had been mostly educated to give for charitable purposes and could not change their outlook overnight. They could not believe that if the state would meet the relief needs, Jews, like other voluntary contributors, would relax in their own giving. Nor did they stop to think that cultural activities had been carried along by campaigns for funds which had emphasized relief needs. If the latter lessened it was to be expected that giving would lessen. And this is precisely what happened. Smaller sums became available for communal needs. Relief activities did not suffer materially because they were supplemented from other sources. But educational, recreational, cultural and national agencies suffered severely. In many instances their inclusion in federation budgets was questioned, with the result that they were either eliminated or their allowances were drastically reduced. Having thrown in their lot with the federations during prosperous times they were in no position to strike out independently at a time when it was more difficult than ever to raise funds. They, therefore, accepted the inevitable, reduced their activities, frequently to the point of diminishing returns, and hoped for a better day.

B. Attitudes Toward Jewish Social Work

This was not altogether due to a lack of funds, important a factor as that was. Much more important was the attitude of Jewish social workers, and the lay leaders whom they influence, toward Jewish social work.[103] While, strictly speaking, it may be inaccurate to speak of an "attitude," for there is probably no single attitude that would be characteristic of all, since there is no formulated philosophy of Jewish social work that would be acceptable to all, any one who knows the situation from first-hand experience and observation knows that not all Jewish social workers are fired with any very great zeal for their work. Nor are they even thoroughly convinced about its necessity, purpose, goal, function, motivation, or future. Some there are who question its value, its justification, its efficacy, and the need for it. They look upon it as a hold-over from an earlier day when it had its justification and need in the isolation of the Jew and when it served also to aid in the survival of the group. Since group survival is not their aim and since isolation is no longer the case and may also be considered undesirable, they can see little justification for it.[104]

Nor can they see anything distinctively Jewish in Jewish social work. This is particularly true of those who are doing the different types of case work. With the greater professionalization of social work and the greater interchange of views and experience between Jewish and non-Jewish social workers due to community chest and other influences, Jewish case workers became more professionally and less Jewishly conscious than their older colleagues were. This meant that they became more interested in the so-called "techniques" of treating their clients than in the "whys" and "wherefores" of their work or in developing the distinctive approaches to it. Jewish social work became "social work for," or at best, "with Jews."[105] Challenging themselves and being challenged by their non-Jewish colleagues for a *raison d'être* of their work, they gradually abandoned the uncritical acceptance of the work, concepts, and philosophies they had inherited. Since no acceptable philosophies were available and since it was easier to do so, they accepted the view that Jewish social work is a hold-over, a vestigial organ, once of useful function, but becoming less significant and meaningful with the passage of time and greater Jewish inter-penetration, co-mingling, and participation in the common life.

This view was strengthened by the influx of large numbers of college-trained men and women who were accustomed to think of social problems in general economic or sociological terms and who had neither the interest, knowledge nor inclination to seek out or develop for themselves a specifically Jewish point of view. It became fashionable to question the Jewish aspects or values of Jewish social work. The leaders sought contacts with non-Jewish social workers, first, because it is the natural thing to do, second, because non-Jewish recognition means enhanced status in the Jewish group. A by no means negligible factor in this process was the fact that non-Jewish social work, because of its size, differentiation, and greater degree of professionalization, had something to offer which the Jewish group lacked—technical consideration of case work problems on a professional level. Hence they sought non-Jewish affiliation. The pace set by the leaders or executives was eagerly followed by staff members, for the same forces operated with them, plus the natural tendency to imitate and emulate one's chief. This was the ruling attitude among case workers except in the very few instances where the executive was interested in, or sought to develop, the Jewish aspects of case work. But these were so rare that their influence was insufficient to stem the tide.

The situation is somewhat different among federation executives. The very nature of their work forces them to think and speak in terms of "the Jewish Community." Although it may be doubted whether many federation executives have a very clear idea as to what they mean by "the Jewish Community"[106] they constantly speak about and some undoubtedly come to believe in it. "The Jewish Community" is for them a sort of anthropomorphic being. They

speak of it as if it possessed the human attributes of thinking, feeling and willing. It has wishes and desires, it approves
and disapproves, it grants and withholds its bounty as it is
satisfied or dissatisfied with given programs, procedures
and practices. Jewish social work becomes to them an
expression of this rather mystical "Community."

But even they, who are under constant pressure to think
and formulate the larger and perhaps more fundamental
purposes and values of Jewish social work, have produced
little that may be considered a guide for those who may
wish to develop a philosophy of Jewish social work in the
United States. Whatever has been written is in the most
general terms.[107] Nothing has thus far come even from this
group which the more specialized social workers might apply
to their own work. There are instances where specialized
workers who were not particularly known for their interest,
zeal or advocacy of the Jewish phases of social work became
active propagandists for a so-called Jewish emphasis when
they became federation executives. On the other hand,
there are some rather notable instances where federation
executives, who argued in and out of season for a specifically
Jewish social work and the application of Jewish values to it,
abandoned all attempts at such applications on leaving the
federation field.

More recently, within the past three or four years, a new
factor has arisen in the field of Jewish social work, which
threatened to become the most disorganizing of all—the
radical activities of the younger group of Jewish social workers. These consist mainly in the organization of what amounts

to industrial unions of all employees in Jewish social agencies and in carrying on a type of propaganda which characterizes radical groups and movements. The causes for this development may be found in the economic and social background, education, and experience of a great many of the workers; in the absence of a well-defined philosophy of Jewish life and of Jewish social work in the United States; in a loss of confidence in the lay and professional leadership; in the stresses and strains induced by social work during the depression; in a belief that much if not most of the maladjustment with which social workers have to deal has an economic base and can only be adequately treated through a readjustment or reorganization of the economic basis of society;[108] and finally in a series of reductions of salaries of employees of Jewish social agencies since the depression. The last may well be considered the precipitating cause, for it was the opposition to salary reductions and efforts to obtain reinstatement of the original salaries that brought the movement to the fore and gave the heterogeneous elements which composed it the feeling of common interest and purpose necessary for a successful movement.[109] Members of this group look upon themselves as "workers." They secured a charter from the American Federation of Labor. Efforts to get them to view Jewish social work as a profession devoted to "social services," incompatible with the conflict philosophy and methods of labor organizations and especially the more radical ones, and the peculiar and special responsibility that rests or should rest upon Jewish social workers to act responsibly in order not to bring discredit upon the Jewish group, are scorned and ridiculed. Their interest is in the larger group. The Jewish problem, to them, in so far as they give it any thought at all, is an expression, a function, of the general economic problem and will be solved only when the problems of the total population are solved. Hence their emphasis on the larger scene. This movement is not limited to New York City, although the leading group is to be found there. Similar groups with similar interests and activities are to be found in other large cities.[III]

Quite aside from the inevitable diffusion in interest and effort with respect to Jewish social work as such, which this movement means, it affects Jewish social work adversely in the loss of interest and good-will on the part of Jewish lay leaders. It has also induced unfriendly attitudes in non-Jewish social workers and their leaders toward Jewish social work and Jewish social workers. Although some of the most important leaders of the movement are non-Jews, the facts that it had its origin as an organized endeavor in the Jewish group, and that some prominent Jewish social workers are among its leaders, have served to identify the Jewish group with its activities.

In the past year or two, a new and in some respects oppositional group came into being among the younger Jewish social workers which bids fair to become popular, as its ideals and principles become better formulated and wider known. The basic philosophy of this group is that of Labor Zionism. While they support the trade-union interest and approach of social workers, they oppose what they consider the assimilationist tendencies of the more radical social work group as well as other Jewish groups. They differ from the ordinary Labor-Zionists in their search for a program which would emphasize Jewish life in America without neglecting the upbuilding of Palestine. In ideology they are closely related to the adherents of the "Reconstructionist" philosophy of Jewish life.[112]

C. Effect on Jewish Social Work

These are some of the forces now at work. It is doubtful whether, with the exception of the last named group, they promise the most wholesome development of Jewish social work or Jewish life. They have in fact already served to weaken both in many directions, if not to undermine them. We need only look at the present status of some of the functional fields to see how true this is.

Enough has been said in the foregoing pages to indicate the seriousness of the situation for the family welfare societies and indeed for all case work agencies. Though this type of social work is in no immediate danger from the lack of a clientele that needs to be served, or even from a lack of funds, it faces grave dangers from within and without. In its failure to develop a distinctive philosophy and approach to its work, in its failure to discover and emphasize the Jewish or cultural aspects of its work; in its turning over to the public agencies large numbers of its clients to be handled by untrained or inadequately trained people with low standards of work; in the loss of many of its trained and experienced workers to the public agencies; in the radical

attitudes and activities of some of its workers, Jewish family
care or case work appears to be losing ground, prestige, and
the compelling appeal it had for the Jewish public. Whether
it is called upon to take back a large number of those who
are now being handled by the public agencies, (not an impossible development in view of the known attitudes of important public officials and spokesmen of the large taxpayers
and recently adopted policies regarding relief on the part
of the Federal government) or whether it eventually settles
down to the handling of only those who are ineligible to
public funds, Jewish family work will probably have a more
difficult time to justify itself in the future than it has had
in the past. There will seem less justification for the maintenance of separate Jewish family societies because of what
has transpired during the last few years. Unless they develop
a *raison d'être* that will be sufficiently compelling in word
and deed to make a critical and unwilling contributing
public realize that in supporting them they are maintaining
a service that is essential and has a distinctive contribution
to make to the general as well as the Jewish community,
Jewish family case work agencies, and for that matter, all
Jewish agencies, may suffer a severe set-back in their program and activities.

That the Jewish family care agencies are aware of some
of these problems and are trying to deal with them, goes
without saying.[113] But it may be doubted whether they
have thus far analyzed and faced them in fundamental
terms. Such analysis would have to include not only the
quantity and quality of their work and the adequacy of the

support rendered them by federations, but also what their function and scope should be in a scheme of Jewish community organization. It should answer the questions how they are prepared to meet their problems as Jewish agencies, and how they differ from the general case work agencies, public and private, which may serve as large if not larger numbers of Jewish clients than do the Jewish agencies.

Unless they succeed in doing this and find a real justification for themselves, it is not impossible that they will be destroyed. In fact they now carry in themselves the seeds of their own destruction. For in addition to the factors already outlined, many case workers, case work executives, and board members have assimilationist tendencies. Some are convinced assimilationists. This is especially true of some of the board members. They are frequently encouraged by the case work group to look upon Jewish agencies and their work as separatist endeavors which should be discouraged. It is but a step from the adoption of such a philosophy for general Jewish agencies to its execution in the agencies with which they are associated. Family agency executives holding such views do not see the consequences to their own work. But, here as everywhere, the tragedy is that it will not be they alone who will suffer from their blindness, but the entire Jewish community. (See pp. 49–50).

The institutional phases of social work, such as the agencies for the care of the sick, the aged, and children, are in a somewhat better position.[114] While they were all affected by the depression and the factors outlined, they suffered less, comparatively, than did the other types of work, especially the educational and recreational agencies. The latter were and, in some instances, still are in a most precarious state. They were the hardest hit of any of the fields of Jewish social work. They not only lost ground but had to fight for their very existence. And it cannot be said that the struggle is over. The same may be said of the national agencies. It will depend upon how long this depression will last and upon the rate of recovery whether these agencies, especially those that have a cultural program, will survive or not. If they survive it is likely to take a long time before they will reach once again the position they occupied, or the quality of work they did at the onset of the depression.

But it is the federations that are facing the greatest challenge and severest test. Many factors conspired to weaken them. Federations, as a rule, obtained their greatest power through the purse rather than from the sanctions resulting from constructive and representative leadership. With a more limited purse has, therefore, come a diminution of power and influence. Federations have been accused of being arbitrary, undemocratic, near-sighted, timid or cowardly, visionless, interested mainly in charity, leaderless, provincial, mechanical in their approach and method, dominated by an assimilationist point of view, being supported by and appealing to comparatively small numbers, and as having failed to develop the cohesiveness, organization, and other characteristics of an intelligent, wisely planned and representative Jewish community. While all these charges cannot be leveled at all federations, it must be admitted that most federations have some of these shortcomings, and that some of them would have to plead guilty to most or all of the charges if they had the necessary objectivity and insight to see themselves as they are seen by others.[115]

There is some evidence that some of the more thoughtful lay and professional federation leaders are becoming increasingly aware of the shortcomings and dangers faced by federations. Some beginnings have been made in the direction of a re-examination of the purpose, function, scope, method, form of organization, and future of federation.[116] While such soul-searching as is taking place in federation may be expected to yield constructive results, one cannot expect too much since the patient, himself, does the examining, the diagnosing, the prescribing, and the treating. Indeed, the very factors responsible for their defects may easily prevent federations from viewing themselves as they are and may nullify, in large measure, the efforts at reorganization. But be that as it may, it is freely admitted that the federation is not the Jewish community, and that it would have to be fundamentally reconstructed if it were to become *the* Jewish community. The Community Councils, discussed elsewhere, represent one attempt at creating such a representative Jewish community organization. But they have some of the vices of their virtues and may perhaps even threaten the very structure of federations unless they are wisely planned and even more wisely conducted.

Nevertheless, when all is said and done, federation is the most important single organization in the Jewish community. It has in it elements of strength, at least potential strength, which no other organization in the Jewish community has. In its representativeness, unrepresentative as it is; in its community-mindedness, narrowly conceived as it may be; in its financial resources, limited as they are; in its leadership, one-sided and conservative as that may be; in its catholicity of interests, circumscribed as they are said to be; and in its status before the non-Jewish world, there lie possibilities heretofore unrealized and assuredly unequalled by any existing Jewish organization in the United States. How to tap these resources and how to convert the federation into the comprehensive community organization which seems to be the present need and which, better than any other existing organization, it can become, is the problem. Indeed, this is the greatest need faced by Jewish social work. In a sense it is the central problem of Jewish community organization in the United States.

CHAPTER XII

KNOWLEDGE AND LEADERSHIP IN JEWISH COMMUNAL ACTIVITY

A. Scientific Knowledge and Community Planning

The thoughtful reader will have been impressed with what must appear as the planlessness of Jewish social work in the United States. The fact that this is not peculiar to social work but characterizes all American Jewish life does not mitigate the evil. Nor does it lessen the need for adequate planning in Jewish social work. Indeed, here if anywhere, one should expect to find wise planning based on a long range view of trends and tendencies, as well as the present and future needs of the Jewish community. That this is not the case will be clear from all of the foregoing. This is due to a multitude of causes, not the least of which is the lamentable absence of basic and dependable knowledge concerning Jewish life in America. Planning requires knowledge, and there is little if any knowledge regarding the significant aspects of Jewish life in America.

Strange and unbelievable as it may seem, and sad a commentary on American Jewish communal leadership as it may be, the fact remains that the rudimentary and basic facts needed for sound community planning are not available. Activities which cost almost one hundred million dollars annually are carried on by agencies and organizations throughout the country. But there are no generally accepted standards, norms, or criteria, based on careful inquiry and study which could serve as touchstones to test existing activities and programs or for planning new activities. There is no agreement anywhere on what is necessary or how things might be done best. Agencies and communities do their work along traditional lines. Most of their activities and practices have no more justification than the opinion of some that they are needed and should continue. These opinions are usually founded on little more than personal experience, valuable and unreliable as that may be, and *laissez-faire* attitudes. New agencies, institutions and organizations come into being without adequate study. Few, outside of those actually faced with the problem, seem to realize that it is inconsistent with intelligent community planning that important enterprises should be built and vast sums of money spent on so inadequate a basis.[117]

Not only is there no knowledge for determining existing needs and how to meet them, but what is of even greater importance, there is no knowledge which would help obviate the mistakes of the past. Even in the training of the future leaders of Jewish communal activity little more can be done at the present time than to acquaint them with the experience, opinions and practices of their predecessors.[118] The fact that few of them had the kind of educational and professional preparation which would enable them to test their experience and accumulate a body of knowledge, scientifically gathered and examined, and therefore scientifically dependable, seems to trouble no one. Nevertheless it must be clear that this may make for a perpetuation of practices and procedures which should and would be abandoned if the necessary knowledge based on scientific research were available. It must be equally clear that unless such knowledge is developed the Jewish communal worker of the future cannot be prepared as he should be and his work cannot be based on the solid foundation of fact.

Local community programs are not the only sufferers because of this lack. Important national and international projects are likewise rarely based on research and study. They are usually launched because of the interest of aggressive and vigorous personalities. Leadership in them is limited to comparatively few outstanding persons who are so busy and harassed with the many demands made upon their time and the many responsibilities forced upon them, that it is impossible for them to be intimately informed on all the aspects and ramifications of the enterprises they sponsor. Leadership is usually based on personal influence, wealth, position, but rarely on intimate and factual knowledge. Decisions on important and far-reaching projects are reached without the basic consideration they should receive. Objectivity and scientific examination of facts as a basis for action are practically unknown. National and international work is no better off than local work, if indeed it is as well off, from the standpoint of the availability of knowledge on which it should be founded.

Nor is the situation different with respect to the broader aspects of Jewish life. There is no information on the role of the Jew and the Jewish community in American life.

No one knows what the tendencies are or should be for the best development of Jewish life, for its complete expression and harmonious adjustment with the non-Jewish community. Lamentations are frequently heard about the decline of the synagogue and temple, the Jewish home, the Jewish school, and the disintegration of the Jewish community.[19] No one can say definitely that the decline and disintegration are actually taking place. Nor does anyone know what forces are responsible and how they might be controlled. There is no lack of opinions as to what is the prevailing situation. But the facts are unavailable.

The depression forced many to a recognition of the precarious position of the Jew in the economic life of the nation. But no one can say definitely what the situation actually is, what the trends are, what to do and how to do it in order to exercise some measure of control over the situation. Nor is it known what factors make for existing discrimination against Jews in the social, economic, and academic fields. Yet Jewish life and welfare would seem to depend upon accurate knowledge and intelligent control of these forces.

B. Types of Knowledge Needed

At various points in this survey some of the types of knowledge necessary for effective work were suggested in connection with the discussion of the activities which should be based on them. While it is not intended here to outline a detailed program of research for developing this knowledge, it may be helpful, for purposes of summary and clarification, to enumerate the broad fields of study needed. The most important of these may be grouped under four heads: 1. Studies in Jewish social life and practice; 2. Studies in Jewish social change; 3. Studies in Jewish social backgrounds; 4. Research for Applications.

1. *Studies in Jewish Social Life and Practice.* This field includes such studies as would throw light on Jewish social groupings, their bases, their common elements, and their differences; Jewish social organizations such as philanthropic, religious, cultural, educational, protective, nationalistic, social, mutual benefit, and politico-economic organizations; and Jewish social institutions such as the family, the synagogue, the school. These studies should supply objective and factual description of these and other phases of Jewish life. The information thus gathered would serve two essential needs: it would supply the data necessary for establishing the needed norms in Jewish life; it would reveal the attitudes and motivations which are all important in dealing with human beings.

That a knowledge of norms, attitudes and motivations, is essential for understanding, planning, and controlling social life will be clear to anyone who is at all informed on the subject. Unless we know what is normal, even though that norm may change, we have no basis for judging the adequacy or inadequacy of any practice. Nor do we know what to strive for. In like manner, unless we have some knowledge of attitudes and motivations, any attempt to control social life and action is doomed to failure even before it is begun.[120]

2. *Studies in Jewish Social Change.* These studies should aim at discovering and ascertaining the trends and tendencies in Jewish life. Intelligent community planning is impossible without basic knowledge concerning the trends in Jewish population; extent, need, and validity, of existing philanthropic, religious, and educational activities; Jewish participation in industrial, commercial, academic and professional pursuits; the trends in Jewish assimilation and anti-Semitism. As we have seen, (Chapter I) very little is known regarding the Jewish population, its distribution, its birth rate, morbidity, and mortality. Planning programs which depend upon a knowledge of population factors, will continue to be impossible for the Jewish people so long as it is ignorant about these factors.

We have seen, also, (Chapters VI–X), that Jewish philanthropic activities are undergoing marked changes. All types of prognostications have been made as to the future of Jewish philanthropy in this country. Some believe that Jewish relief activities will disappear for various reasons and propose that the Jewish community concentrate its efforts on cultural activities. Few would agree as to just what these should be, although many are convinced as to the wisdom of their particular proposals. Some would have the Jewish community take full advantage of available state subsidy for dependents; others are fearful of the effects of such a policy. Some would do away with orphans' homes; others, perhaps no less informed, think that orphans' homes still constitute an important aspect of child care. The relation of the Jewish Federations to the Community

Chests and the effects of the latter are pressing problems. The role, development, and future possibilities of the Community Center are subjects of much concern to a large number of communally minded persons. The relation between national, international and local needs is an aggravated problem. These and scores of other questions and problems need study and research. They cannot and will not be effectively solved without dependable knowledge, knowledge which can be accumulated only through research.

The changes which are taking place in the religious life and activities of the Jewish group have been a subject of much speculation during the last decade or so. It has been charged by friends and foes alike that Jews are non-religious, if not irreligious; that the synagogue and temple no longer attract even the old, much less the young; that the Rabbinate is disintegrating, and that the programs of organizations concerned with the furtherance of Jewish religious life are groping blindly and are carrying on their work unintelligently; that the orthodox and conservative synagogues prepare their members for the reform temples and that the latter prepare them for ethical culture, Christian Science, and Christianity; that Rabbis are trained not for the problems which they face in the modern community, but along lines which give them a knowledge of the past, little appreciation of the present, and no preparation for the future. Careful, painstaking, scientific inquiry into these and other problems would be of incalculable value to the welfare of Jewish religious life.[121]

The same may be said for the educational activities of

the Jewish community. Large sums of money are spent annually, and some would say ineffectively, on Jewish education. Many Jewish communities are puzzled about the type of Jewish education that should be given their children. Programs have been formulated and school systems organized with very little more than the conviction of one or at best a few aggressive and strong personalities. A more necessary and fruitful subject for scientific inquiry so far as the Jewish community is concerned, can hardly be suggested.

Closely associated with Jewish religious and educational life and activities is the question of assimilation. Are the Jews assimilating to their environment, or are they unassimilable, as they have been charged? What sound indexes can be developed, with special reference to assimilation rates of other racial and cultural groups? In a sense, all far-sighted community planning has to take this factor of assimilation into account.

Changes are commonly believed to be taking place in the Jewish group with respect to employe-employer relationship. It is believed that the Jew is fast disappearing as an employe in certain trades and occupations in which he once held a dominant position, e. g. the needle trades. Are these changes actually taking place? What do such changes portend? What can be done, if anything should be done, to direct these changes? What about Jewish participation in the commercial and industrial life of the country? Even the most superficial inquiry will quickly reveal the extent of our ignorance on this subject. Social workers, rabbis and others are frequently called upon to give vocational advice and assistance to young people and their parents without having any of the knowledge upon which to base the advice. Community leaders are troubled about the problem of directing Jewish youth to a sounder economic distribution. But they have nothing more than their own individual opinions, biases, prejudices, and perhaps vested interests, to guide them in their expressions and activities.

A problem of deep concern to those in close touch with American Jewish academic life is the extreme difficulty (one might almost say the impossibility) of Jews entering academic life. Despite their interest, preparation, and willingness to make the sacrifices which academic work demands, positions in universities for Jewish young men and women seem almost out of reach. While there are some outstanding Jewish scientists and academicians in some of the leading universities throughout the country, the belief is universal that it is folly for any Jew to attempt to strike out for an academic career. To what degree is this true, and what are the facts? It is obvious that if Jewish young men and women become convinced that an academic career is impossible for them, it will not be long before they will abandon the effort, and we shall have the anomaly of the "people of the book" becoming "the bookless people." It may be safely predicted that the very people who now keep Jews from academic life will be all too quick to charge the Jewish people with crass materialism and with making no contribution to the intellectual life of our country. As evidence they will cite the fact that Jews are not partici-

pating in academic pursuits. The fact that they were kept
from these pursuits will be no argument, precisely as the
facts that Jews were not permitted to own land and were
not admitted to the Guilds in the Middle Ages, do not
prevent the charge that the Jews are parasites, and are not
productive in the basic necessities of life. Before efforts
can be made at controlling and modifying this situation,
the facts must be known. They are not now to be had.

It has been charged from time to time that the Jews are
crowding the professions, especially those of medicine and
law. Charges have also been made frequently that they
constitute an undue proportion of those that indulge in
unethical practices. These professions seem to be over-
crowded. Vocational and educational guidance might be
of great help and value here. Wise and far-visioned Jewish
leadership would seem to require knowledge for planning
and control. But if one is to judge by what is being done
about the matter, Jewish leadership is hardly aware of the
problem, its importance, and the extent of our ignorance
concerning it.

Finally, anti-Semitism. What are the trends and tendencies in anti-Semitism? Is the position of the Jew in
American life today safer than it was a decade or two ago,
or less safe? What is the effect of Hitlerism on non-Jewish
American opinion and what may the results be ultimately?
What can be done about it? Such knowledge is essential
to the welfare of the Jewish people. Together with the
knowledge of what anti-Semitism is and how it may be
controlled, knowledge is needed, also, as to how extensive

it is, whether it is on the increase or decrease, and where the outbreaks may be expected.

3. *Studies in Jewish Social Backgrounds*. In addition to the factual information on current life and practice and the trends and tendencies in the Jewish community, it is necessary also to study the origins and development of the practices, groupings, and institutions in the Jewish community in order to explain them. Studies of backgrounds could make profound contributions to the understanding of attitudes and motivations, and would no doubt make clear the reasons and causes for the changes observed and described, as well as the reasons for existing differences and conflicts and how to deal with them.

The types of knowledge outlined above would provide a basis for determining the needs of the Jewish community and how to go about to meet them. Knowledge of this type would give the Jewish leaders the means for intelligently controlling and directing Jewish communal development in so far as this may be done. It would give direction to the present activities, so that they might best serve the purposes for which they are designed, and would indicate the changes which should take place for more effective community organization. Such studies would go a long way to aid Jewish community leaders and Jewish communities as a whole to avoid current errors, inefficiency, and waste. Who knows but that such calamities as may be impending might not also thus be avoided!

4. *Research for Applications*. The fourth type of research suggested above is concerned with the problem of develop-

ing the applications of such knowledge as may already be in existence, to the practical problems faced by the social practitioners, be they lay or professional. The existence and possession of knowledge by no means signifies the ability to apply it. Such applications must be worked out through careful, painstaking experimentation which should partake, in so far as possible, of the methods obtaining in the laboratory, with suitable controls. While life cannot be controlled and simplified to the extent that the scientist can control and simplify his problems in the laboratory, the accuracy and dependability of the findings will depend very largely, if not entirely, on the degree to which such experimentation in life will approximate experimentation in the laboratory. Such work requires not only a body of dependable knowledge, but workers who will have sufficient faith in science and scientific methodology to be willing to undertake to work at the applications. Once they have been developed, they can be tried and checked by the practitioners in the field with further modifications and refinements being developed on the basis of the experience of the practitioners. It is only through a procedure of give and take of this kind that sound practice can be developed. Without this cooperation between pure scientist, applied scientist or technologist, and practitioner, the practice must remain on an empirical basis and costly and dangerous mistakes are unavoidable.[122]

The foregoing enumeration suggests a few of the more important types of knowledge needed for long time planning. Many problems indigenous to American Jewish life or which may arise out of the European situation have only been mentioned in passing. Thus nothing has been said about the effect upon the American Jewish community of the continuous collections of large sums for overseas purposes whether for relief and reconstruction or Palestine upbuilding. Nor has mention been made, except by implication, of the lack of a comprehensive program for Jewish life in this country. Organizations whether large or small, local, national, or international, are, with few exceptions, primarily interested in their own immediate programs and how to obtain the funds for their work. None is charged or has charged itself with the formulation of a sound program for Jewish community development. Local agencies engage in what frequently amounts to a tug of war for funds from their federations. The federations engage in a similar struggle with the national agencies to retain as much money as possible for local purposes. The national agencies compete with each other, for as great a share for themselves as the traffic will bear. And so it goes year in year out: local needs and interests against national needs; national agencies against each other. Rarely if ever is the community as a whole considered. Nor is the direction in which it should be developed known or clearly envisaged. That this is important and should be faced is obvious. The only question is whether community effort should continue on the empirical basis characterizing most of the activities at the present time or whether it should be based on knowledge obtained from scientific inquiry.

It would be outside the present scope and purpose to

discuss the auspices under which these studies should be conducted. It is important to indicate, however, that there exists no agency for the effective performance of this task. As has been pointed out, American Jewry which spends approximately one hundred million dollars annually on local, national, and international activities has thus far not had the vision, wisdom, or intelligence to spend even one-tenth of one per cent on inquiries which would yield indispensable information for making the large expenditures serve the most useful purpose. It is almost inconceivable that at a time like the present when research and scientific knowledge play so large a role in all commercial and industrial enterprises, they should play so unimportant a role in communal enterprises. The failure to place these activities on the most valid scientific basis possible is probably the best index to what the situation is. It is a sad commentary not only on the quality of work done but on the leadership which sponsors it.

C. Knowledge and Leadership

It would be difficult to say whether adequate knowledge or far-sighted leadership is more important for the type of communal planning which would be equal to the existing requirements and would anticipate possible future needs. In a sense they depend upon each other. Certainly they would reinforce each other. It is pertinent, therefore, to examine next the type and quality of leadership in Jewish communal work in the United States.

As has already been indicated, it is commonly assumed

that any local or national enterprise depends for its success on the type of sponsorship which it is able to obtain. Hence it is the usual practice to seek out the most prominent or wealthiest persons, locally or nationally, and to interest them in the project to be undertaken. If the promoters are able to interest one or more very prominent persons the rest is easy. The less prominent are usually ready if not eager to associate themselves with the enterprise because of the prestige of the others. The best known in the group are given the positions of leadership, responsibility, and authority in the organization. Here lies one of the greatest dangers to Jewish community development and leadership. The prominent persons have so many duties and responsibilities, that it is physically and mentally impossible for them to devote the necessary time to each of the enterprises with which they are connected. With the best intentions in the world, they cannot be intimately informed on the manifold activities to which they lend the prestige of their names.

The foregoing should not be misunderstood to disparage the contributions or importance of lay leadership. No one who worked intimately with the late Felix M. Warburg and Julius Rosenwald, and knows from first hand experience, as does the writer, their whole-hearted devotion to communal problems, could fail to appreciate the great value of such leadership. But this appreciation should not blind one to the tremendous burdens and responsibilities which such men carry or the magnitude of the problem of securing an intelligent and thoroughly informed lay leadership.

The desire to obtain wealthy and well known persons to sponsor organizations, while in itself very desirable, gives rise to several evils, chief of which are the exclusion from boards of persons who though perhaps less prominent and less wealthy, have the knowledge and experience which could be of most value to the organization; and the concentration of leadership and control in the hands of a comparatively small group. A study of board memberships of the important Jewish organizations would show a large degree of interlocking directorates. Board members are selected almost exclusively because of their influence, ability to contribute or to obtain financial contributions from others, or because they are personally known to influential board members. Nevertheless, leadership, authority, and responsibility rest in the hands of board members. How to select people who will have the necessary knowledge, vision, courage, and capacity for leadership, for the many and difficult tasks facing the Jewish communities throughout the country is indeed an important problem.

Thus far comparatively little effort has been made to utilize those people in the community whose business it is to be informed on the questions coming before the different boards. Except for those problems which are of a business nature where business men have a special contribution to make, professional men, physicians, attorneys, rabbis, educators, social workers, psychologists, sociologists, economists, labor leaders, etc., all have knowledge, information and experience which would stand communities in good stead. The community would be immeasurably enriched if they were wisely used.

In the last decade or two there has been greater appreciation than ever before of the need for trained professional leadership for Jewish communal effort. Such leadership is gradually being provided through a graduate professional school for Jewish social work. The graduates of this School and other schools are assuming important positions and will no doubt supply a higher type of leadership than could have been possible without this facility. They will become the career men of the Jewish community of the future.

A wise and well organized community will eventually realize that the problems of Jewish life are much too complex to be safely left to untrained persons, or those who can devote only a limited amount of time and energy to them. It will therefore place a premium on training for community service.[123]   It will also recognize that provision must be made either on a local or national basis to endow leadership so that those who are professionally engaged in community service may be able to afford the luxury of courageous, frank, honest, speech and action. If, in addition, provision will also be made for developing the information and knowledge outlined in the preceding pages and to secure a courageous and well informed lay leadership, a beginning will have been made toward creating the type of Jewish community organization and activity which a large, wealthy, intelligent and enlightened people should have.[124]

CHAPTER XIII

SUMMARY

1. *Size of Jewish Population.*—It is estimated that there are approximately 4½ million Jews in the United States and that they constitute about 3½% of the entire population. No accurate figures are available because no religious question is included in the Federal census, made every ten years. Such substitute methods as are used are neither very accurate nor entirely satisfactory. Information available from these substitutes indicates that the Jewish population is concentrated in the larger cities. Thus, cities of 100,000 population and over have 84% of the Jewish population, whereas they have only about 28% of the general population. Estimates of growth of Jewish population in the United States indicate that in the present century it has increased by almost 450%.

2. *Jewish Economic Distribution.*—Information regarding the economic distribution of the Jews is no more reliable or satisfactory. Such sample studies as have been made indicate that the Jews are concentrated in the light industries, in commerce, and the professions. They are very sparsely represented in the heavy industries. A survey by *Fortune*, one of the leading periodicals in the United States, reveals that Jews do not control any of the fields which they are commonly assumed to dominate. The article concludes that "Jews do not dominate the American scene. They do not even dominate major sectors of the American scene."

There is considerable occupational discrimination against Jews. Some of the large industrial organizations have practically no Jews working in them. Discrimination is felt also in the professions, more especially medicine, law and teaching. While American Jewish leaders have been concerned with the problem of a more equitable occupational distribution, no concerted or effective action has thus far been taken.

3. *Anti-Semitism.*—Anti-Semitism has been on the increase in the last half dozen years. Although it is estimated that there are approximately 50 anti-Semitic organizations in the United States, there has thus far been no unity of action among them. Nor is there at the present time any organization that functions on a country-wide basis. Anti-Semitism has received no support or backing from the local or Federal governments. Nevertheless, there are factors in the American situation, especially since the depression and Nazi propaganda, which could easily be utilized against the Jews. While there are some safety factors against anti-Semitism in the make-up of the American population, the situation is such as to give some people cause for uneasiness. This despite the fact that official relations between Jews and non-Jews are friendly and that there are some organizations whose purpose it is to foster inter-racial and inter-religious co-operation.

4. *Attitude Toward Immigration.*—This country is gradually abandoning the traditional policy of being a refuge for those suffering from religious and political persecution. Immigrants are not wanted. Although this is not altogether

a new policy, it has been emphasized since the depression. In the last two or three years, despite a generous attitude on the part of high government officials, representatives in the Congress of the United States have urged shutting the doors against immigrants. In this they are supported by labor organizations on the theory that immigrants would take away jobs, already too scarce, from Americans. Since many millions of Americans are still unemployed this argument finds favor with the general population.

An analysis of the immigration figures reveals that in the years 1881 to 1936 about 2,500,000 Jews came to the United States; that they constituted about 9% of the total immigration; and that they came here with the intention of settling permanently as evidenced by the relatively high proportion of women and children, and the low proportion of emigrants and deportees.

The problem of adjusting the immigrants was serious among Jews and non-Jews. Gradually, however, the spirit of intolerance against the foreigner gave way to an attitude of sympathetic understanding and encouragement of group and cultural loyalties. But the early misunderstandings and differences between the immigrants and the older settlers in the Jewish community left their imprints. These are observable at the present time in some phases of organized Jewish life.

One of the problems arising out of the large Jewish immigration is that of Jewish adjustment to American life. Three programs are distinguishable with respect to their attitude toward Judaism, nationalism, and group survival.

They may be roughly classified into the three following groups, although they are not organized as such: (1) religionists; (2) culturists; (3) assimilationists.

5. *Religious Organization.*—Religiously the Jewish population in the United States may be grouped under three categories: (1) Those who have broken away from traditional Judaism and its practices and are affiliated with Reform temples, where men and women sit together with bare heads, with mixed choirs and organ music; (2) Those affiliated with conservative synagogues, institutions where a good many traditional practices are still adhered to, not so much because they were ordained by God as because they are part of the traditions of the Jewish people; (3) Those who adhere strictly to traditional forms and practices and are affiliated with Orthodox synagogues. There are many who are not affiliated with any religious institutions but find their Jewish affiliation through non-religious activities, such as charity, Zionism, etc.

Each of the religious groups has its own organization, with its affiliated Brotherhoods and Sisterhoods, Sunday Schools, activities for its youth, training schools for Rabbis, and programs for adult education. It is estimated that between 300,000 and 350,000 Jews are directly affiliated with religious institutions. and that between 1,250,000 and 1,500,000 are indirectly affiliated because they belong to families that belong to some religious organization.

6. *Educational Activities.*—American Jews are as a rule averse to the creation of parochial schools. Jewish children attend the public schools and have more than their propor-

tional representation in the elementary and secondary schools, colleges and universities.

In the field of Jewish education there are the traditional educational forms and institutions. However, while there are still the *Talmud Torahs*, *Hedarim*, and private *Melamdim*, they are no longer as important as they were. This is largely due to a movement to modernize Jewish education which began about a quarter of a century ago. There are now Boards of Jewish Education, affiliated with the federations of charities in most of the large cities, with modern facilities in terms of buildings, teachers, supervisors and curricula. In the last few years this movement has been subjected to considerable criticism and some antagonism. This was partly due to the depression and partly due to differences of opinion regarding what Jewish education should be. The effect of this opposition cannot yet be evaluated.

7. *Organizations for Civic Protection.*—The problem of civic protection is handled mainly by four organizations, The American Jewish Committee, the American Jewish Congress, the Anti-Defamation League of the B'nai B'rith, and the Jewish Labor Committee. These four organizations, though having the same purposes, differ in method and approach. Although the four represent a fair cross-section of the entire Jewish population, no one organization represents all sections of the Jewish community.

8. *Organizations for Local Social Service.*—The Jewish communities in the United States have a variety of organizations for social welfare, each functioning in its own sphere.

The problem of poverty and dependency is handled by

about 100 organizations which are doing what is called "case work." They aim not only to supply the financial needs of families and individuals in want, but to rehabilitate them through various means, such as establishment in business, vocational retraining, etc. These organizations are highly professionalized. During the depression they suffered from an enormous increase of case loads and expenditures, and later by a great reduction of work due to the development of public relief programs. During the height of the depression they spent between four and five million dollars a year, and handled about 30,000 Jewish families annually. These organizations are invariably part of the federations for Jewish charity and secure their funds from them. In some instances they also secure funds from non-sectarian sources.

The health care of the Jewish people has been attended to by a number of hospitals throughout the country. Each of the larger communities has one or more hospitals. There are about 70 Jewish hospitals in the country, some of them ranking among the foremost institutions of their kind in the United States. They spend approximately 19 million dollars a year and give about 2¾ million days care to Jewish and non-Jewish sick. There are also a number of clinics and special hospitals for chronic diseases, tuberculosis, etc. The financial needs of the hospitals and family care agencies constituted for many years the largest burden on the Jewish federations. In recent years because of the relief program of the Federal Government, the family societies have taken fourth place in the total amount they spend annually.

Dependent children have been cared for by child care agencies and orphans homes, of which there are approximately 100 in this country. About 10,000 Jewish children receive care in these institutions, of which there are several types. There are: first, the congregate type, a large institution which houses all the children; second, the cottage type, which aims to recreate a family atmosphere in a cottage caring for about 20 children of both sexes and all ages, presided over by a cottage mother; and third, the foster-home type of care. This latter is based on the theory that children require a home atmosphere for their best development. Children are, therefore, boarded out in private homes for a given sum per week or month, and presumably take their natural place with the other children in the home.

There are a number of Jewish organizations supplying facilities for adult education and recreation. The most important of these are a large number of institutions called Jewish Community Centers, although some are known under different names. It is estimated that there are between 300 and 400 such organizations in the United States, and that approximately 300,000 young men and women are affiliated with them. These institutions have a central national organization, the Jewish Welfare Board, which had its origin during the World War. This organization serves as a clearing house for the institutions and provides educational material for their programs. Between 30 and 40 million dollars have been spent in the last two or three decades on buildings to house the activities of the various types of Jewish centers. There are other organizations serving the needs of adult Jewish education. Among these may be mentioned the B'nai B'rith, which, through its Hillel Foundations, located in a number of colleges and universities throughout the country, reaches the Jewish college youth. The Young Judea aims to interest the Jewish youth in the Jewish people and to give them a better understanding of its history and future. This organization has about 750 clubs with a total membership of about 20,000. There are about 25 similar organizations for Jewish youth with similar purposes. But it cannot be said that there is a Jewish youth movement if by that is meant a well-planned and co-ordinated country-wide activity. Each of the youth organizations acts independently and is responsible only to its own leaders.

The problem of the aged, though not very large, still has need for about 50 institutions to care for the old people. They are usually part of the federations and are supported by them. The Federal program of old-age pensions may seriously affect this type of work.

The social work activities in the Jewish community are, in most instances, united in a federation of Jewish charities. This type of organization had its beginning at the close of the last century and has developed enormously. There are at the present time about 70 such federations throughout the country. At first they were merely the money collecting and distributing agencies for all the charitable organizations in the community. In the last decade or so they have aimed to become, in addition, the planning and co-ordinating agencies for the social service needs in the Jewish community.

The Jewish federation has stimulated the creation of the Community Chest, an organization which is to the general community what the federation is to the Jewish community. Community Chests, which are to be found in most of the cities in the country, have in turn influenced the Jewish federations and Jewish social work in important ways. The majority of Jewish federations in cities where there are Community Chests, are members of the Chests and receive their funds from them. This has frequently militated against the best development of Jewish social work because the standards of Jewish giving and Jewish work are in many instances higher than in the non-Jewish community. The existence of the Community Chest and Jewish participation in it has tended to level down the quality of work. The Community Chest has frequently given opportunity to Jews, who had their training in the Federation, for outstanding leadership. This is one of the ways in which Jews have made important contributions to the non-Jewish community in the social service field.

Community Chest participation influenced the creation of another central organization in the Jewish community, namely, the Welfare Fund. This was due to the fact that Community Chests could not support distinctively Jewish activities, such as Hebrew schools, and various non-local, national and overseas organizations. There are now between 25 and 30 Welfare Funds in the country which spend approximately one million dollars a year. It is estimated that federations and welfare funds spend a total of about fifty million dollars annually.

9. *Organization for Non-Local Social Service.*—There are a large number of national agencies, by which is meant organizations which serve the country as a whole rather than a particular locality. Among the most important of these are: the national hospitals for tuberculosis; the B'nai B'rith, a fraternal organization with a large educational and social service program; the Jewish Telegraphic Agency, a news-gathering and distributing organization; The Graduate School for Jewish Social Work, a graduate institution for training Jewish social workers, authorized to grant the Master's and Doctor's degrees; The Council of Jewish Federations and Welfare Funds, the co-ordinating organization for federations and welfare funds; The National Conference of Jewish Social Welfare, the national organization of Jewish social workers; the National Co-ordinating Committee for German Refugees, an organization aiming at facilitating the adjustment of German immigrants; the German Jewish Childrens Aid, an organization which is bringing over and placing German Jewish children; the Hebrew Immigrant Aid Society, an organization serving Jewish immigrants; The National Desertion Bureau, an agency which locates deserting husbands; and a variety of others, including those already mentioned in connection with the work for civic protection and adult education. They obtain their funds either in part or in whole from federations, welfare funds, membership fees, and individual contributions.

Among national agencies which do their work overseas

the largest is the Joint Distribution Committee, which, since its organization in 1914, has done work in 42 countries and spent more than $84,000,000. Its main work has been in Poland, Russia and Palestine. Another organization functioning overseas is the ORT. This organization is primarily concerned with supplying vocational training in various European countries. These and other similar organizations also get their funds from federations and welfare funds. The Refugee Economic Corporation was organized a few years ago to aid German refugees through immigration and colonization.

There are a large number of organizations in the United States working for Palestine. The most important of these are: The Zionist Organization of America, which carries on a program of educational propaganda for Zionism; The American Palestine Campaign, which is the fund-raising instrument through the United Palestine Appeal, for the Jewish Agency for Palestine, The Jewish National Fund and other Palestine organizations; The Hadassah, or Women's Zionist Organization of America, which has functioned mainly in the field of health in Palestine, and undertook, more recently, in conjunction with the American Jewish Physicians Committee, the creation of a post-graduate medical school in the Hebrew University; The American Friends of the Hebrew University; the National Labor Committee for Palestine; the Mizrachi Palestine Fund, etc. It has been estimated that between four and five million dollars a year are spent by American Jewry for overseas work.

In the current year (1937) the Joint Distribution Committee and the United Palestine Campaign are each campaigning for $4,500,000.

10. *Other Activities.*—In addition to the foregoing organizations and activities there are many organizations functioning in the social, cultural and political spheres. Among these are the less formal relief societies, usually composed of women; family societies which are clan organizations bearing the names of particular families and providing various social and insurance benefits for their members; fraternal organizations and *landsmanschaften* which also have some social and insurance features; libraries, publication societies, and cultural activities. There are very few permanent political organizations. During election campaigns the different political parties create temporary organizations to advance the interests of their candidates. But the Jewish community discourages distinctly Jewish political activity.

11. *Present Tendencies.*—The foregoing outlines the most important Jewish organizational activities in the United States. The depression has brought a serious challenge to most of them. But the greatest challenge has come to the national agencies, the family welfare organizations, and the federations. The national agencies suffered because of lack of funds. Local communities have felt that existing funds should be mainly utilized for local needs. Appropriations to national agencies have therefore been seriously reduced and in some instances entirely eliminated. Some of them were forced to curtail their work almost to the vanishing point.

The family welfare agencies have suffered from the depression, first, because of a lowering of standards due to the unprecedented demands made upon them, and later by the development of public welfare programs which have raised questions as to whether they have a continuing function to perform. More important than this, however, has been the attitude of some Jewish social workers, especially the younger group, who have no particular convictions about Jewish life, Jewish social work or social work in general, and have been active in the larger scene, frequently to the detriment of Jewish social work and Jewish life in this country. Federations have been challenged on the ground that they are not truly representative, since they receive their main income from and are controlled by comparatively small numbers; that they are arbitrary and limited in point of view, and are not really the type of Jewish community organization which Jewish life in America needs. While some federation leaders are aware of these criticisms and limitations, and experiments are being made to create a more representative and comprehensive Jewish community organization, these experiments have not yet gone far enough for a safe prediction as to their future.

12. *Knowledge and Leadership.*—There is practically no comprehensive planning of Jewish community activity in the United States. Nor is there the type of knowledge needed for wise and intelligent planning. Organizations and agencies carry on their work on the basis of tradition. Despite the dangers inherent in the situation there is little if any awareness of the need of fundamental knowledge

about the various aspects of Jewish life. Such knowledge is not likely to be developed until special facilities are created for its accumulation. Leadership is concentrated in comparatively few persons and is based on prestige, position, influence, wealth, and willingness to serve but rarely on knowledge and special competence. The professional groups such as physicians, attorneys, rabbis, social workers, economists, sociologists, psychologists, are not used on the boards of the enterprises where their knowledge could be utilized. There is a greater appreciation today than formerly that the problems facing Jewish life require special knowledge and equipment for their solution, and that it is not safe to leave them to those who can devote only part of their time and energy to them. It is becoming increasingly clear that Jewish communities will have to make provisions for career men who will be adequately trained for the manifold tasks and responsibilities which will come to them. To some extent such persons are being made available through the existence of a graduate school for training Jewish communal leaders. Little has thus far been done, however, to create the means for accumulating the necessary basic knowledge without which all work, whether professional or lay, is more or less ineffective.

NOTES AND REFERENCES

NOTES AND REFERENCES

I

[1] The number reporting Yiddish as their mother tongue were: for 1910,—1,051,767; 1920,—1,091,820; 1930,—1,222,658. They represented 8.0%, 8.2% and 9.1% of the foreign white population in the respective censuses. See Frank, H.: "Yiddish in America", *The Zukunft*, Vol. XLII, No. 2, February, 1937, pp. 75–80. It is interesting to note in this connection that whereas there were almost 1,000,000 Jewish immigrants between 1910 and 1930, most of them coming from eastern Europe where Yiddish is spoken, there was an increase of only about 170,000 who gave Yiddish as their mother tongue during the same period.

[2] Linfield, H. S.: "The Jewish Population in the United States 1927," *American Jewish Year Book*, Vol. 30, 5689, pp. 101–108.

[3] Engelman, Uriah Z.: "The Need for Jewish Population Statistics," *The Menorah Journal*, Vol. XIII, No. 5, November 1927, pp. 467–478; Lurie, H. L.: "Some Problems in the Collection and Interpretation of Jewish Population Data," *The Jewish Social Service Quarterly*, Vol. X, No. 4, June 1934, pp. 263–268. See also Engelman, Uriah Z.: *The Jewish Community in Figures, Guess-Work and Speculation That Pass for Statistics*, New York, The Jewish Information Bureau, 1937.

[4] For the history of the Industrial Removal Office (I.R.O.) see Bogen, Boris D.: *Jewish Philanthropy*, New York, Macmillan, 1917, pp. 113–122; Joseph, Samuel: *The History of the Baron de Hirsch Fund*, Philadelphia, The Jewish Publication Society, 1935, pp. 184–205; and Margolis, Rose: *History of the Industrial Removal Office*, Thesis, The Graduate School for Jewish Social Work, New York, 1935.

For the Galveston Movement see Waldman, Morris D.: "The Galveston Movement," *The Jewish Social Service Quarterly*, Vol. IV. No. 3, March 1928, pp. 197–206. Also Joseph, Samuel: *Op. Cit.* pp. 205–210.

[5] McGill, Nettie Pauline: "The Religio-Cultural Backgrounds of New York City's Youth," *Better Times*, published by the Welfare Council of New York City, Vol. XVIII, No. 27, April 1937, pp. 22–28.

[6] The figures for 1818 to 1927 are based on Linfield, *op. cit.*, pp. 157–158. The 1935 figure is based on the estimate of Jacob Lestchinsky: "The Number of Jews in the World," *Jiwo Bleter*, Vol. IX, No. 4–5, April–May, 1936, p. 166.

II

[7] Glück, Elsie: "Jewish Workers in the Trade Unions," *Jewish Frontier*, Vol. II, No. 14, December 1935, pp. 11–15. See also Adler, Evelyn: *The Union Backgrounds, Relationships, and Activities of Selected Members of the International Ladies' Garment*

Workers' Union, New York, 1933, Master's Thesis, The Graduate School for Jewish Social Work, 1937.

[8] *Jews in America,* by the Editors of Fortune, New York, Random House, 1936. Reprinted from *Fortune,* Vol. 13, No. 2, Feb. 1936.

[9] Linfield, H. S.: "The Communal Organization of the Jews in the United States, 1927," *American Jewish Year Book,* Vol. 31, 5690, p. 203. In the reprint of this article issued under the same title in 1930 by the American Jewish Committee, this information appears on p. 129.

[10] Kinzler, Esther: *Some Aspects of the Occupational Distribution of Jews in New York City as Revealed Through a Study of Selected Groups of Names in the New York City Directory for 1933,* Thesis, The Graduate School for Jewish Social Work, New York, 1935.

[11] *Ibid,* Table 111, p. 209.

[12] *Ibid,* Table 112, p. 210.

[13] A number of studies are under way at the Graduate School for Jewish Social Work aiming at securing reliable figures on population and economic distribution in smaller communities. The following community studies, either in process or completed for the Master's degree, are available in the Library of the School: Langer, Marion: *A Study of the Jewish Community of Easton, New York, 1933;* Fleischman, Abraham: *A Study of the Jewish Community of Staten Island, New York, 1936-1937;* Meyer, Lena: *A Study of the Jewish Community of New London, Conn., 1936-1937;* Ryckoff, Irving: *A Study of Organizational Affiliations and Activities of the Jewish Population of Staten Island, New York, 1936-1937.*

The Conference on Jewish Relations, The Jewish Welfare Board and the Bureau of Jewish Social Research are also working in this field. It is hoped that through the combined efforts of these and other organizations the necessary data will be secured. See *infra,* pp. 117 for descriptive statements of these organizations.

[14] Kinzler, *op. cit.,* Table 115, p. 216.

[15] *Ibid,* Table 116, p. 219.

[16] Davidson, Gabriel: "The Jew in Agriculture in the United States," *American Jewish Year Book,* Vol. 37, 5696, pp. 99-134. The *Annual Report of the Jewish Agricultural Society for 1936,* gives a good picture of the current situation. For a statement of the Work and achievements of the National Farm School see reports by the National Appeals Information Service and the Council of Federations and Welfare Funds, New York, 1929 to 1935.

[17] Cohen, Morris R.: "Jews in Commerce and the Professions," *Proceedings,* National Conference of Jewish Social Service, 1934, pp. 21-28.

[18] Strauss, Israel: "A Medical School Associated with a Jewish Hospital," *ibid,* 1932, pp. 179-184.

[19] Rubinow, I. M.: "Jews Without Jobs," *Jewish Frontier,* Vol. II, No. 2, December,

1934, pp. 17–18; "Economics of Anti-Semitism," *ibid*, Vol. II, No. 4, Feb. 1935, pp. 19–22; "Middle-Class into Proletariat," *ibid*, Vol. II, No. 6, pp. 10–14.

[20] Broun, Heywood and Britt, George: *Christians Only*, New York, The Vanguard Press, 1931. See also *Jews, Jobs and Discrimination, A Report on Jewish Non-Employment*, by J. X. Cohen, published by the American Jewish Congress, New York, 1937; and Ramelson, Sylvia L: *A Study of the Help-Wanted Advertisements in New York Newspapers, 1928, 1931, 1935*, Thesis, The Graduate School for Jewish Social Work, New York, 1936.

[21] Selekman, Ben: "Planning for Jewish Economic Welfare," *Proceedings*, National Conference of Jewish Social Service, 1934, pp. 28–33; Rubinow, I. M.: "The Economic and Industrial Status of American Jewry," *Proceedings*, National Conference of Jewish Social Service, 1932, pp. 28–38; Feldman, Herman: *Racial Factors in American Industry*, New York, Harper & Bros., 1931; Symposium on "Jewish Economic Adjustment Problems and Programs," *Proceedings*, National Conference of Jewish Social Service, 1935, pp. 7–43; Valentin, Hugo: *Anti-Semitism*, Chapter 17, "The Jews and The 'Productive' Industries," New York, The Viking Press, 1936, pp. 278–299; Lasker, Bruno: "Jewish Handicaps in the Employment Market," *Jewish Social Service Quarterly*, Vol. II, No. 3, March 1926, pp. 170–177; Lasker, Bruno (Editor): *Jewish Experiences in America*, New York, The Inquiry, 1930; Symposium on "Jewish Vocational Service Agencies," *Jewish Social Service Quarterly*, Vol. VIII, No. 1. Sept. 1936, pp. 198–221.

III

[22] *American Jewish Year Book*, Vol. 38, pp. 545–548. The problem of Christian-Jewish relationships is dealt with in the following books: Clinchy, Everett R.: *All in the Name of God*, New York, John Day Company, 1934; Silcox, Claris Edwin and Fisher, Galen M.: *Catholics, Jews and Protestants. A Study of Relationships in the United States and Canada*, New York, Harper, 1934; Baker, Newton Diehl, Hayes, Carleton J. H. and Straus, Roger Williams: *The American Way, A Study of Human Relations among Protestants, Catholics and Jews*, Chicago, Willett, Clark & Company, 1936.

[23] Waldman, Morris D.: "The International Scene in Jewish Life," *Proceedings*, National Conference of Jewish Social Service, 1932, pp. 19–25; and see especially, *id.*: "Problems Facing the Jews Throughout the World and Their Implications for American Jewry," *ibid*, 1934, pp. 54–56.

[24] See discussion under Civic Protection (pp. 62–66 and note 45.)

[25] Cf. Park, Robert E. and Miller, Herbert A.: *Old World Traits Transplanted*, Chicago, Society for Social Research, University of Chicago, 1925; Drachsler, Julius: *Democracy and Assimilation. The Blending of Immigrant Heritages in America*, New York, Macmillan, 1930; Berkson, I.: *Theories of Americanization With Special Reference to the Jewish Group*, New York, Teachers College, Columbia University, 1920; and Miller, Herbert A.: *Races, Nations, and Classes*, Philadelphia, Lippincott, 1924.

IV

[26] Davie, Maurice R.: *World Immigration with Special Reference to the United States.* New York, Macmillan, 1936, pp. 367–385.

[27] The *visas* for immigration to the United States amounted to only 11% and 13%, respectively, of the quotas alloted to the major countries for 1935 and 1936. See *Bulletin d'Information de la HIAS-JCA Emigration-Association*, (HICEM), No. 13, May 1937, p. 12.

[27a] Tables 12 to 15 inclusive are based on data contained in different sources but especially in Joseph, Samuel: *Jewish Immigration to the United States from 1881 to 1910*, New York, Columbia University Press, 1914, and the issues of the *American Jewish Year Book*, 1910–1937.

[28] For characteristics of Jewish immigration, see Joseph, Samuel: *op. cit.*, pp. 127–148.

[28a] Cf. Karpf, M. J.: "The Relation Between Sociology and Social Work," *The Journal of Social Forces*, Vol. III, No. 3, March 1925, pp. 1–8; and "The Development of the Relation Between Sociology and Social Work," *Publications of the American Sociological Society*, Vol. XXXI, 1927, pp. 213–222. For a list of the Americanization studies see the fly leaf in *Old World Traits Transplanted*, by Park, Robert E. and Miller, Herbert A., New York, Harper & Bros., 1921.

[28b] The best statement of this general position is contained in *Old World Traits Transplanted* by Park and Miller, cited above. The numerous references to auto-biographical material and studies of immigrant attitudes will be of great value to an understanding of the problem of immigrant adjustment. The background of the Americanization problem, its significance for America and the immigrants, and needed reforms, are outlined with admirable lucidity and insight by Julius Drachsler in *Democracy and Assimilation*, New York, Macmillan, 1920.

[28c] The reluctance of Jewish immigrants to abandon their customs and habits and the problems arising therefrom, are described by George Wolfe in *A Study of Immigrant Attitudes and Problems Based on an Analysis of 400 Letters to the "Bintel Brief"*; the differences, conflicts and accommodation between Jewish immigrants and the older settlers are outlined by Harold Silver in *Some Attitudes of East European Jewish Immigrants Toward Organized Charity in the United States, 1890–1900*, Master's Theses, The Graduate School for Jewish Social Work, New York, 1933 and 1934 respectively.

[28d] The Orthodox-Religionist point of view is presented in *The Jewish Library*, edited by Leo Jung, New York, Bloch, 1928, 1930, 1934. Its opposition to both, secular nationalism and Zionism, is outlined by Isaac Breuer: *The Jewish National Home*, Translated by Miriam Aumann, Frankfort, A.M., J. Kauffmann, 1926, pp. 21–32. A favorable position toward nationalism and Zionism is presented in the *Mizrachi Jubilee Publication of the Mizrachi Organization* of America (1911–1936), Edited by P. Churgin and Leon Gellman, New York, 1936.

The attitudes of Reform Jewry can be traced in the various issues of the *Yearbook*,

Central Conference of American Rabbis and especially Vol. XLV, 1935, pp. 260–312. For characteristic presentations of the anti-nationalist point of view among the Reform Rabbinate see: Schulman, Samuel: "Israel," *ibid.*, pp. 291 ff. and Lazaron, Morris S.: *Judaism's Message to the World,* 1937.

The attitudes of the Conservative wing are recorded in the *Proceedings of the Rabbinical Assembly of the Jewish Theological Seminary of America.*

[28e] The culturist and non-religious theoretical basis of cultural pluralism in the United States with special reference to the Jewish group is developed by: Berkson Isaac B.: *Theories of Americanization. A Critical Study with Special Reference to the Jewish Group,* New York, Teachers College, Columbia University, 1920; Kallen; Horace M.: *Culture and Democracy in the United States; Studies in the Group Psychology of the American Peoples,* New York, Boni and Liveright, 1924, and *Judaism at Bay. Essays Toward the Adjustment of Judaism to Modernity,* New York, Bloch, 1932, which contains a vigorous criticism of the religious point of view and procedure. The nationalist Zionist point of view is clearly set forth in *Rebirth, A Book of Modern Jewish Thought,* edited by Ludwig Lewisohn, New York, Harper, 1935; the *New Palestine* and in the various Zionist publications.

The non-Orthodox, (Humanist) religious-nationalist viewpoint is best presented in the writings of the Reconstructionist group among which the following are the most representative: Kaplan, Mordecai M.: *Judaism as a Civilization,* New York, Macmillan, 1934, and the abridgement thereof by Ira Eisenstein: *Creative Judaism,* New York, Behrman's, 1936; Kaplan, M. M.: *Judaism in Transition,* New York, Covici Friede, 1936; *The Jewish Reconstructionist Papers,* edited by Mordecai M. Kaplan, New York, Behrman's, 1936; Goldman, Solomon: *A Rabbi Takes Stock,* New York, Harper, 1931; Kohn, Eugene: *The Future of Judaism in America,* New Rochelle, N. Y., The Liberal Press, 1934; Dinin, Samuel: *Judaism in a Changing Civilization,* New York, Teachers College, Columbia University, 1933; and *The Reconstructionist,* New York, a periodical.

The secular-nationalist viewpoint must be considered in relation to its European background. The best expositions may be found in the following: Oscar I. Janowsky in *Jews and Minority Rights,* New York, Columbia University Press, 1933; Abraham G. Duker in "Theories of Ber Borochov and Their Place in the History of the Jewish Labor Movement" in Ber Borochov: *Nationalism and the Class Struggle, A Marxian Approach to the Jewish Problem, Selected Writings,* New York, Poale Zion-Zeire Zion of America and Young Poale Zion Alliance of America, 1937. The change in the ideology of this group can be best traced in the periodicals, *Jewish Frontier* and *Labor-Zionist News Letter,* both published in New York. In contrast to the Labor Zionist groups with their increasing interest in the American Jewish community and their acceptance of the English language as their medium of expression is the Yiddishist secular-culturist movement. Summaries of their points of view may be found in "The Problem of

Yiddishism" by Abraham G. Duker, *The Reconstructionist*, Vol. II, No. 20, February 5, 1937, pp. 7–10, and *An Introduction to the Yiddishist Movement in the United States* by Clement Staff, Thesis, The Graduate School for Jewish Social Work, 1937.

[28f] The assimilationist non-religious and anti-religious viewpoint may be traced in the following: Isidor Lazarus, "In Defense of the 'Accidental' Jew," *The Menorah Journal*, Vol. XVI, No. 4, April, 1929, pp. 335–345; Morris R. Cohen, "As a Liberal Views It," *Proposed Roads for American Jewry, A Symposium*, New York, National Council of Jewish Women, 1936, pp. 51–79, also his "A Plea for Liberalism," *Proceedings*, The National Conference on Jewish Welfare, 1935, pp. 56–58; and Gessner, Robert: *Some of My Best Friends Are Jews*, New York, Farrar & Rinehart, 1936, Chapter XXV, "The Scapegoat Must Choose," pp. 349–371.

The Assimilationist viewpoint of those intimately identified with Jewish Communal work has not been as clearly or as vigorously stated as some of the others. This is probably due to the inherent inconsistencies between these views and communal work. Suggestive though incomplete statements may be found in the following: Lurie, Harry L., Director, the Bureau of Jewish Social Research, now the Council of Jewish Federations and Welfare Funds, *Proceedings*, the National Conference of Jewish Social Service, 1933 and 1934, pp. 26–27 and 111–113 respectively; Anonymous: "Facing Reality" in Symposium "What Makes Jewish Social Work 'Jewish'?", *Jewish Social Service Quarterly*, Vol. VII, No. 1, September 1930, p. 15. A liberal, and extremely tolerant viewpoint, not altogether dissimilar from the assimilationist position, characteristic of many intelligent lay leaders in Jewish communal work, is presented by William J. Schroder, President of the Council of Jewish Federations and Welfare Funds, *Proceedings*, National Conference of Jewish Social Service, 1934, pp. 30–31.

V

[29] For a comprehensive survey of the activities of the Union of American Hebrew Congregations, see *The Sixty-Second Annual Report*, issued June 1936.

[10] This information was obtained in conversation with the director of the organization. For a statement of the activities of the United Synagogue, see the Report of the National Convention of the United Synagogue of America, Washington, D. C. March, 1936, *The United Synagogue News*, Vol. 1, No. 2, April, 1936.

[31] Linfield, H. S.: "Jewish Congregations in the United States," *American Jewish Year Book*, Vol. 30, pp. 199–200.

[32] Levinger, Lee J.: "Surveying the Jewish Students," *B'nai B'rith Magazine*, Vol. 51, No. 7, pp. 214, 234–35; id., *The Jewish Student in America*, The B'nai B'rith Hillel Foundation, Cincinnati, Ohio, 1937.

[33] That this is considered something of a problem will be clear from the following quotation taken from Silcox, Claris Edwin and Fisher, Galen M.: *Catholics, Jews and*

Protestants, A Study of Relationships in the United States and Canada, New York, Harpers, 1934, p. 217.

"Of all the religious bodies the Jews alone have refrained from establishing institutions of higher learning. Their only colleges have been primarily theological, such as the Hebrew Union College in Cincinnati, the Jewish Theological Seminary of America in New York, Dropsie College in Philadelphia and The Yeshiva College in New York which recently began to do work of collegiate grade. Jewish students attend not only the state and non-sectarian institutions, but also the various institutions connected with Christian denominations, both Protestant and Catholic. There is some feeling, both in Jewish and Gentile circles, that it might be desirable for the Jews to develop institutions of their own, especially since many private institutions have sought to establish a *numerus clausus* for Jews. In one of the largest Catholic universities in the East 56.7% of the student body consists of Jews."

[34] An excellent description of the older types of Jewish education is contained in Gamoran, Emanuel: *Changing Conceptions in Jewish Education. Book One. Jewish Education in Russia and Poland*, New York, Macmillan, 1925.

[35] The most comprehensive recent general summary on Jewish education is the article by Israel Chipkin, "Twenty-Five Years of Jewish Education in the United States," in the *American Jewish Year Book*, Vol. 38, pp. 27–116. Also issued separately by the Jewish Education Association of New York City, 1937.

[36] Benderly, Samson: "Jewish Education in the United States," *Proceedings of the 1935 Conference on Jewish Welfare*, pp. 40–42.

[37] Dushkin, A. M. and Honor, Leo L.: "Aims and Activities of Jewish Educational Organizations in America," *Jewish Education*, Vol. V, No. 3, Oct.–Dec. 1933, pp. 136–146.

[38] Cf. Karpf, Maurice J.: "To What End Jewish Education," *The American Hebrew*, Vol. CXL, No. 16, March 5, 1937, pp. 948–968; also Chipkin, *op. cit.*, (reprint) pp. 103–112.

[39] Lehrer, Leibush: "The Jewish Secular School," *Jewish Education*, Vol. 8, No. 1, Jan.–Mar. 1936, pp. 33–42. Also *Jewish Social Service Quarterly*, Vol. XII, No. 3, March 1936, pp. 308–317.

[40] Karpf, Maurice J.: "A Decade of Jewish Philanthropy," *B'nai B'rith Magazine*, Vol. 46, Feb. 1932, p. 146.

[41] The American Jewish Committee: *Twelfth Annual Report*, New York, 1919, p. 45.

[42] On the date of organization, popular election, functions and adjournment of the first Congress, see *The American Jewish Congress, What It Is and What It Does*, published by The American Jewish Congress, 1936, pp. 7–8. Also, pp. 8–9 for organization, purpose and democratic nature of second Congress. While reference is made to a popular election in June 1917, for the first Congress which adjourned in accordance with "the

terms of the agreement creating the Congress," and to the convening of the second Congress in June 1922, no mention is made of a democratic election either at that time or subsequently. For the history and activities of the American Jewish Committee and the American Jewish Congress on behalf of minority rights during the World War see: Janowsky, Oscar I.: *The Jews and Minority Rights,* New York, Columbia University Press, 1933, especially pp. 174–190; 264–268.

[43] *Proceedings of the Fourteenth General Convention of the Constitution Grand Lodge (Changed to Supreme Lodge) B'nai B'rith Held in Washington, D. C. May 4 to 8, 1935.*

[44] Gebiner, B.: "The Jewish Labor Committee, Its Establishment and Work," (in Yiddish) *2nd Annual Convention of the Jewish Labor Committee,* October 27th, 1935, New York, 1935, pp. 13–25.

[45] For the latest discussion of this problem, see: Lurie, Harry L.: "Is Jewish Unity Possible?" *The Menorah Journal,* Vol. XXIV, No. 3, Oct.–Dec., 1936, pp. 219–227; Kaplan, Mordecai M.: "Is Jewish Unity Possible?" *ibid,* Vol. XXV, No. 1, Jan.–March, 1937, pp. 128–131; Lurie, Harry L.: *"A Rejoinder," ibid.* pp. 131–133.

For a different approach to the problem see Waldman, Morris D.: "Jewish Morale in the Present Situation," to appear in the *Proceedings,* National Conference of Jewish Social Welfare, 1937, pp. 37–42.

VI

[46] This table is based on Table 1, p. 1, *1935 Year Book of Jewish Social Work,* Part II, issued by The Council of Federations and Welfare Funds, New York, November, 1936. For analysis of expenditures of local, national and overseas agencies see also Tables 2 and 3, pp. 4 and 6 respectively of the Year Book.

[47] Karpf, M. J.: "Toward a Source-Book on Jewish Philanthropic Origins" In three parts. Part I, "Biblical Conceptions of Charity," *Jewish Social Service Quarterly,* Vol. XII, No. 3, March 1936, pp. 324–336; Part II, "The Talmudic Period," *ibid,* No. 4, June, 1936, pp. 396–410; Part III, "Biblical Excerpts on Benevolence," *ibid,* Vol. XIII, No. 2, Dec. 1936, pp. 297–303.

[48] Karpf, Maurice J.: *A Social Audit of a Social Service Agency,* published by the Jewish Social Service Bureau of Chicago, 1925, Section 8, "Family Rehabiliation Through Independence, the Self-Support Department," pp. 109–125. See also, Leavitt, Moses A.: "The Self-Support Department of the J.S.S.A." in *Handicapped Wage Earners,* published by the Jewish Social Service Association, New York, 1928, pp. 32–38. For an enthusiastic evaluation by a non-Jew of this type of work, see Bruno, Frank J.: "A Romance of Family Case Work, a Review of a Social Audit by Maurice J. Karpf," *The Survey,* Vol. LV, No. 2, October 15, 1925, pp. 87–89.

[49] Clarke, John J.: *Social Administration Including The Poor Laws,* Isaac Pitman and Sons, London, 1922, p. 24.

[50] Additional material on traditional attitudes and practices of Jewish Charities will be found in: Schechter, Solomon: "Notes of Lectures on Jewish Philanthropy," *Studies*

in Judaism, Third Series, Philadelphia, Jewish Publication Society, 1924, pp. 238–276; Bogen, Boris D.: *Jewish Philanthropy*, New York, Macmillan, 1917; Frisch, Ephraim: *An Historical Survey of Jewish Philanthropy . . .*, New York, Macmillan, 1924; Cronbach, Abraham: "The Me'il Zedakah," *Hebrew Union College Annual*, Vol. XI, 1936, pp. 503–567; Abrahams, Israel: *Jewish Life in the Middle Ages*, Edward Goldston, London, 1932; Kaplan, Mordecai M.: "Jewish Philanthropy,"in *Intelligent Philanthropy*, edited by Ellsworth Faris and Others, Chicago, University of Chicago Press, 1930.

[51] Karpf, M. J.: "Wanted—A Return to Basic Values," *Jewish Social Service Quarterly*, Vol. VIII, No. 2, Dec. 1931, pp. 59–63.

[52] The facts and figures in this and the next chapter, relating to the period before 1880, are based on material gathered by the writer and his students from the Jewish press, periodical literature and agency reports of the time. The following newspapers were especially helpful: *The Occident*, New York, (1843–1850); *The Asmonean*, New York, (1849–1858); *The Jewish Messenger*, New York, (1857–1902); *The Jewish Times*, New York, (1869); *The Zeitgeist*, (1880–1882).

[53] *Fifty Years of Social Service. The History of the United Hebrew Charities of the City of New York. Now The Jewish Social Service Association, Inc.*, published by the Jewish Social Service Association, New York, 1926. For attitudes of older Jewish settlers toward East European Jewish immigration and immigrants, see Silver, Harold: *Attitudes of the East European Jewish Immigrants Toward Organized Jewish Charity in the United States, in the Years 1890–1900*. Master's Thesis, The Graduate School for Jewish Social Work, New York, 1934.

[54] United Hebrew Charities: *Annual Reports*.

[55] Karpf, M. J.: *A Social Audit of a Social Service Agency*, published by the Jewish Social Service Bureau, Chicago, 1925, p. 41.

[56] Karpf, M. J.: *The Scientific Basis of Social Work*, Columbia University Press, New York, 1931, chapters IV–X, XIII and XIV.

[57] Rubinow, I. M.: "Racial Factors Which Condition Case Work with Jewish Families," *Proceedings*, National Conference of Jewish Social Service, 1924, pp. 22–32; Karpf, M. J.: "The Training School for Jewish Social Work, Its Program, Possibilities and Limitations," *Proceedings*, National Conference of Jewish Social Service, 1925, pp. 11–41. See also "Principles Underlying the Organization of the School," *The Catalogue* of the Graduate School for Jewish Social Work, 1936–1937, Vol. XII, No. 1, pp. 13–16.

[58] Cf. Karpf, M. J.: "Discussion of Racial Factors Conditioning Case Work with Jewish Families," *Proceedings*, National Conference of Jewish Social Service, 1924, pp. 33–36. For a comprehensive treatment of these two fields of knowledge in the sense in which they are referred to here see Park, Robert E., and Burgess, Ernest W.: *Introduction to the Science of Sociology*, Chicago, University of Chicago Press, 1924; and Karpf, Fay Berger: *American Social Psychology, Its Origin, Development and European Background*, New York, McGraw-Hill, 1932.

[59] The interested reader will find a simple exposition of the case work process as practiced in these agencies and its historical development, in "Die Fürsorge für den Einzelfall in Amerika," by M. J. Karpf, in the *Jüdische Wohlfahrtspflege und Sozialpolitik*, Berlin, Sept.–Oct., 1935, Vol. 5 (N. S.) No. 5, pp. 148–156, or its English translation, *Social Case Work in America*, New York, 1936. A more thoroughgoing treatment of the subject will be found in *What is Social Case Work*, by Mary Richmond, New York, The Russell Sage Foundation, 1922. For a comprehensive description of the complexity of problems and work of Jewish family societies, the reader is referred to the works named in notes 53 and 55 above.

[60] These figures are derived from the *1934 and 1935 Year Books of Jewish Social Work*, Part II. While these publications are issued by the same organization, (the Council of Federations and Welfare Funds, New York) the basis for the figures are somewhat different in the two studies. Compare for instance Page 1. of the issues of the respective years on Jewish family welfare statistics; Tables 5, in the respective appendices; and Tables 4 on child care, Pages 11 and 10 in the respective volumes.

[61] Slawson, John: "Care and Treatment of the Problem Child," *Proceedings*, National Conference of Jewish Social Service, 1935, pp. 156–163. See also Bernstein, Ludwig: "Intermarriage and Jewish Social Service," *Jewish Social Service Quarterly*, Vol. V, No. 4, June 1929, pp. 237–241, and Sections 6 and 7, "Behavior Problems of Boys and Girls" in *A Social Audit of a Social Service Agency*, by M. J. Karpf, pp. 89–109.

[62] Maller, J. B.: "The Maladjusted Jewish Child," *Jewish Social Service Quarterly*, Vol. IX, No. 3, June 1933, pp. 285–295, and Vol. X, No. 2, Dec. 1933, pp. 157–162. See also appropriate sections and Tables in *Can Delinquency Be Measured*, by Sophia M. Robison, Columbia University Press, New York, 1936.

[63] See Golub, J. J.: "Diseases Among Jews," *Jewish Social Service Quarterly*, Vol. IV, No. 2, pp. 144–155, Dec. 1927, for a discussion of these diseases. See also Bolduan, C. and Weiner, L.: "Causes of Death Among Jews in New York City," *New England Journal of Medicine*, Vol. 208, No. 8, Feb. 23, 1933, pp. 407–416, the best available study of Jewish mortality. See also Weiss, Hiram B.: "A Suggestion for a Health Program for a Jewish Community," *Proceedings*, National Conference of Jewish Social Service, 1924, pp. 150–164; Harrison, Frances N.: "A Health Program for a Jewish Community," *ibid*, pp. 164–167.

[64] See *The Asmonean*, Vol. XV, No. 17, Feb. 6, 1857, p. 133; and *The 83rd Annual Report* of the Mt. Sinai Hospital of the City of New York for the year 1935.

[65] See sections dealing with health in the volumes of the *Year Book of Jewish Social Work* for 1934 and 1935.

[66] Slawson, J. and Moss M.: "Mental Illness Among Jews," *Jewish Social Service Quarterly*, Vol. XIII, No. 4, June 1936, pp. 343–350. See also Malzberg, Benjamin: "New Data Relative to Incidence of Mental Disease Among Jews," *Mental Hygiene*, April 1936, pp. 280–291.

[67] Goldsmith, Samuel A.: "Factual Materials in Child Care Surveys of the Bureau of Jewish Social Research," *Proceedings*, National Conference of Jewish Social Service, 1927, pp. 228–240. For some of the results of institutional child care see Bank, Jules: *A Study of 108 Boys Discharged from the Brooklyn Hebrew Orphan Asylum, 1924–1929*, and Goldman, Benjamin B.: *Economic Adjustment of Selected Graduates of the Cleveland Jewish Orphan Home*, Masters' Theses, 1934; and Harris, Dorothy: *Post Institutional Adjustment of 110 Children Discharged from a Child Care Institution, New York, 1934–1935*, Thesis, The Graduate School for Jewish Social Work.

For conflicting viewpoints regarding a program of Jewish education for dependent children see Lurie, Harry and Dushkin, Alexander: "Essentials of a Community Program for Jewish Children," *Proceedings,*, N. C. J. S. S., 1934, pp. 108–118.

[68] Thurston, Henry W.: *The Dependent Child*, New York, Columbia University Press, 1930; Sayles, Mary Buell: *Substitute Parents. A Study of Foster Families*, New York, The Commonwealth Fund, 1936. For a comprehensive history of the development of Jewish child care in the U. S., see Unger, Frieda: *Aims and Methods in the Care of Jewish Dependent Children in the United States*. Master's Thesis, The Graduate School for Jewish Social Work, New York, 1935.

[69] *1935 Year Book of Jewish Social Work*, Part I, p. 7.

[70] Trotzkey, Elias L.: *Institutional Care and Placing-Out*, Chicago, The Marks Nathan Jewish Orphan Home, 1930; and *The Education of Dependent Children. A Survey of the Educational Policies, Practices and Problems of the Three Child Caring Organizations Affiliated with the Jewish Charities of Chicago*, Chicago, 1935 (mimeographed). Also, Dubinsky, G.: "Obstacles in the Development of Foster Family Care for Dependent Children," in *Proceedings*, National Conference of Jewish Social Service, 1923, pp. 370–380. Franklin, Sylvia: *An Analysis of the Histories of the Hebrew Orphan Asylum, New York City, 1935*; and Krems, Jules: *An Analysis of the Case Histories of Children Discharged from Foster Home Care Supervision of the Home Bureau of the H. S. G. S., New York, 1937*, Theses, The Graduate School for Jewish Social Work.

See Karpf, Maurice J.: *The Scientific Basis of Social Work*, *op. cit.*, Chapter IX, pp. 230–250, for a comprehensive discussion on social workers' judgments and criteria regarding the care of children in their own and foster homes.

[71] See *1935 Year Book of Jewish Social Work*, Part II, . . . p. 40.

VII

[72] Seman, Philip L.: "The Place of Character Development Agencies in Our Jewish Social Service Program," *Jewish Social Service Quarterly*, Vol. VIII, No. 1, Sept. 1931 pp. 9–18; *id.*: "The Jewish Spirit in Community Centers," *ibid*, Vol. II, June 1926, pp. 258–264. See also Barron, Harry I.: *A Study of Leisure Time Interests, Preferences and Activities of Children of the Lower East Side of New York City*, Master's Thesis, The Graduate School for Jewish Social Work, 1935.

[73] Jewish Welfare Board: *Activities, 1935, Report of the Executive Director, Harry L. Glucksman*, New York, 1936; and Cohen, Abraham: *Views Regarding Jewish Content in Various Types of Jewish Centers in Relation to Their Aims*, Thesis, The Graduate School for Jewish Social Work, 1936. For a description of the different types of Jewish centers, their scope and function, see Glucksman, Harry L.: "Tendencies in the Jewish Center Movement," *Proceedings*, National Conference of Jewish Social Service, 1923, pp. 144–153.

[74] See *supra*, note 43.

[75] [Young Judea]: *Year Book, 1935–36*, New York, 1936.

[76] See Reports of National Council of Federations and Welfare Funds.

[77] Burstein, Shulamith: *The Status of National Jewish Youth Organizations in the United States—1933–1934*, Master's Thesis, The Graduate School for Jewish Social Work, New York, 1937; Rabin, Florence: *A Study of Programs in Adult Jewish Educational Organizations in New York City, 1936–37*, Thesis, The Graduate School for Jewish Social Work. For a later although incomplete list of youth organizations see Chalmers, M. M.: *Youth-Serving Organizations*, The American Council on Education, Washington, D. C., 1937, pp. 77–91, and additions and comments by A. G. Duker, *The Jewish Social Service Quarterly*, June 1937, Vol. XIII, No. 4, p. 439.

VIII

[78] Hexter, Maurice B.: "Evolutionary Tendencies in the Jewish Federation Movement," *Proceedings*, National Conference of Jewish Social Service, 1926, pp. 9–29; Jacobs, Herman: *Some Aspects of the History of the Federation of Jewish Charities Movement*, Master's Thesis, The Graduate School for Jewish Social Work, 1933; Karpf, M. J.: "A Decade of Jewish Philanthropy," *B'nai B'rith Magazine*, Vol. 46, No. 5, February 1932, pp. 145–147, 158. See also Lowenstein, S., Bernstein, L., Glucksman, H., Goldhamer, S., Goldsmith, S., Hexter, M. B., Kahn, D., Kaplan, H., and Taussig, F:, "Jewish Communal Organization in America," *Proceedings*, National Conference of Jewish Social Service, 1923, pp. 186–199.

[79] National Council of Jewish Federations and Welfare Funds: *Federation Financing of Jewish Social Work in 1934*, pp. 8–13. See especially Table 2, p. 8. The *1935 Year Book, op. cit.*, shows the same trend. See pp. 27–30 and especially Table 17, p. 27.

[80] Mimeographed report issued by the Joint Distribution Committee, New York, December, 1936.

[81] These figures are based on data supplied by Mr. Michael Freund of the Council of Jewish Federations and Welfare Funds. Cf. 1935 Year Book, etc., Part II, pp. 12–13 The figures in the "Year Book" do not correspond to those given here because they are based on different federations and include the income of 27 welfare funds. See

also Freund, Michael: "The Community Chest and Its Influence on the Jewish Community," *Jewish Social Service Quarterly*, Vol. VII, No. 2, December 1930, pp. 30–37; *ibid*, June 1931, pp. 27–32.

[82] Levitsky, Louis M.: "The Story of an Awakened Community," *The Reconstructionist*, Vol. 1, No. 20, February 7, 1936, pp. 7–14; Cohen, Armond E.: "A Year in an Organized Jewish Community," *The Reconstructionist*, Vol. 2, No. 19, January 22, 1937, pp. 12–15; Peiser, Kurt and Boxerman, William I.: *Forward Steps in Jewish Community Organization—Recent Experiences in Detroit*, Jewish Welfare Federation of Detroit, 1936; Weitz, Sidney: "The Significance of the Cleveland Community Council," *Proceedings of the 1937 General Assembly*, Council of Jewish Federations and Welfare Funds, New York, 1937, pp. 10–11.

[83] "Monopoly in Communal Rule," *The Congress Bulletin*, Vol. 3, No. 10, December 1936, pp. 1–4. Simon, Max; Wiesenfeld, Leo: "The Conflict Around the Cleveland Council," *ibid*, Vol. 3, No. 13, January 1, 1936, pp. 3–4.

[84] Karpf, M. J.: "National Service Agencies," *Jewish Daily Bulletin*, New York, April 14, 1935, pp. 3, 8; April 17, 1935, p. 2; April 28, 1935, p. 3. A summary of the foregoing may be found in "Social Service of National Scope," *Proceedings of the National Conference on Jewish Welfare*, 1935, National Council of Jewish Federations and Welfare Funds, Inc. New York, pp. 22–25. For a list of national and overseas agencies receiving assistance from the federations and welfare funds, see *Jewish Social Work Year Book*, 1935.

[85] National Conference of Jewish Social Service and its predecessor, National Conference of Jewish Charities: *Proceedings*, 1900, 1902, 1904, 1906, 1908, 1910, 1912, 1918, 1923–1936; *The Jewish Charities*, 1903–1906; 1910–1919; *Jewish Social Service*, 1919–1921, and its successor, *The Jewish Social Service Quarterly*, 1924–1937.

[86] The Graduate School for Jewish Social Work: *Catalogue*, 1936–1937, listing of theses, pp. 52–64. See also Karpf, M. J.: "Hoichsul far Idishe Sotsiale Arbet in di Fareinigte Shtatn" (A Graduate School for Jewish Social Work in the United States), *Jiwo Bleter*, Vol. V., No. 2, Feb. 1933, pp. 97–108. It should be noted in this connection that there is no organization for Jewish social research as such. The Bureau of Jewish Social Research was in reality an organization for philanthropic surveys. See discussion on Jewish social research, in the *Proceedings*, National Conference of Jewish Social Service, 1928, pp. 109–113; 119–124; and 128–135. The Conference of Jewish Relations discussed below aims to fill this need.

[87] See Karpf, Maurice J.: "Progress and Problems in Social Work Education During the Depression," Presidential Report to American Association of Schools of Social Work, *Jewish Social Service Quarterly*, Vol. 10, No. 4, June 1934, pp. 257–262.

[88] Cohen, Morris R.: Annual Report for 1935. *The Work of the Conference on Jewish Relations*, New York, 1937.

IX

[89] Schneiderman, Harry: "Jewish War Relief Work," *American Jewish Year Book*, 5678, 1917–1918, pp. 194–226.

[90] *Aid to Jews Overseas. Report on the Activities of the American Jewish Joint Distribution Committee for the Year 1935 Including a Brief Resumé for the Year 1936*, New York, 1936.

[91] *Report of the Executive of the Central Board of the ORT Union Submitted to its Primary Session, Paris, September 7–9, 1936.*

[92] *Report of the Administrative Committee to the 39th Annual Convention of the Zionist Organization of America held at the Biltmore Hotel, Providence, Rhode Island, July 4 and continuing through July 7*, 1936. Cf. various issues of *The New Palestine*, A Weekly, published by the Zionist Organization of America.

[93] *President's Report Delivered by Dr. Israel Goldstein before the Annual Assembly of the Jewish National Fund, March 1, 1936.*

[94] Hadassah, the Women's Zionist Organization of America: *Report National Board, Standing Committees and Regional Unit to the 22nd Annual Convention of Hadassah, Philadelphia, October 18–21, 1936.* See also various issues of *Hadassah News Letter*, a periodical, New York, 1936.

X

[95] Karpf, Maurice J., *A Social Audit of a Social Service Agency*, pp. 177–180. See also Palevsky, Mary: "Neighborhood Interference and Cooperation in Case Work with Jewish Families," *Proceedings*, National Conference of Jewish Social Service, 1924, pp. 37–48.

[96] This number is derived from the entries in the list of "Jewish National Organizations in the United States," in the *American Jewish Year Book*, Vol. 38, 5697, pp. 449–512. This figure does not include the number of members of one fraternal order which failed to report them. It includes the 30,000 members of the Jewish Section of the Communist *International Workers Order* which is not listed there. (Cf. Saltzman, R.: *Tsu der Geshichte fun der Fraternaler Bavegung*, New York, 1936, pp. 111, 236.) Data on the various orders can be found in their publications and reports. The Workmen's Circle is the only one of which a complete history is available in English. (Hurwitz, Maximilian: *The Workmen's Circle. Its History, Ideals, Organization and Institutions*, Workmen's Circle, New York, 1936.) Charles W. Ferguson's *Fifty Million Brothers. A Panorama of American Lodges and Clubs*, New York, Farrar & Rinehart, 1937, has a chapter on the Jewish Fraternal Orders (pp. 247–262).

[97] *Jubilee Volume of the Michael Tenzer Family Circle. Tenth Anniversary 1927–1937. A Record of the Activities and Achievements of the Michael Tenzer Family Circle . . .* edited by Solomon Kerstein, New York, 205 p.

[98] Compiled from the entries in the list of "Jewish National Organizations in the United States." *American Jewish Year Book*, Vol. 38, 5697, pp. 449–512.

[99] Kohanski, Alexander S.: *The Yiddish Theater in New York. Season of 1932–1933* Thesis, The Graduate School for Jewish Social Work, New York, 1933.

XI

[100] See Resolutions adopted by the National Conference of Jewish Social Service: *Proceedings*, 1931, Inside Cover and p. 8. See also Goldsmith, Samuel A.: "The Relationship of Jewish Social Work to Public Welfare and Security," *Proceedings of the 1935 National Conference on Jewish Welfare*, published by The National Council of Jewish Federations and Welfare Funds, New York, pp. 19–22.

[101] Cf. Rabinoff, George W.: "Where Is Jewish Social Work Going?" *Jewish Social Service Quarterly*, Vol. IX, No. 2, March 1933, pp. 252–255. See also Taussig, F., Kepecs, J., Dubin, M., Hyman, H. J., and Lurie, H.: "The Effect of the Economic Depression on the Standards of Jewish Social Work Agencies," *Jewish Social Service Quarterly*, Vol. VIII, No. 1, September 1931, pp. 18–33.

[102] Benderly, S., *op. cit.*, note 36.

[103] Kohs, S. C.: "Current Fallacies Regarding Jewish Social Work," *Jewish Social Service Quarterly*, Vol. IX, No. 3, June 1933, pp. 296–305. Cf. Willen, Joseph and Kahn, Edward M.: "Present Trends and Tendencies in the Federation Movement," *Proceedings of the 1935 National Conference on Jewish Welfare*, The National Council of Jewish Federations and Welfare Funds, New York, pp. 26–33. See also Lowenstein, Solomon: "Jewish Needs and Welfare Facilities Today," *Proceedings of the 1936 General Assembly*, The National Council of Jewish Federations and Welfare Funds, New York, pp. 13–17; and Willen, Joseph: "Where is the Money Coming from to Meet Increased Local and Overseas Needs?" *ibid*, pp. 17–21.

[104] See series of articles by Abraham Cronbach, Harry L. Lurie, John Slawson, and Violet Kittner on "What Makes Jewish Social Work 'Jewish' ?" in *The Jewish Social Service Quarterly*, Vol. VII, No. 1, September 1930, pp. 3–14.

[105] Kohs, Samuel C.: "Jewish Content in Jewish Social Work," *Proceedings*, National Conference of Jewish Social Service, 1936, pp. 99–113. See also Schottland, Charles I.: "Social Work as Seen by a Student," *Proceedings*, National Conference of Jewish Social Service, 1929, pp. 189–198; Rose, Joseph: *Changing Objectives and Practices in Jewish Family Welfare Work*, 1934, and Shapiro, Tess: *A Study of Jewish Content in a Selected Number of Case Records of a Jewish Family Agency*, 1937, Thesis, The Graduate School for Jewish Social Work.

[106] Baron, Salo W.: "An Historical Critique of the Jewish Community," *Proceedings*, National Conference of Jewish Social Service, 1935, pp. 44–49; Kaplan, Mordecai M.: "The Organization of American Jewry," *ibid*, pp. 50–73. See especially his *Judaism*

as a Civilization, The Macmillan Company, New York, 1934, Chapter XXI, pp. 280–299.

[107] Rubinow, I. M.: "The Credo of a Jewish Social Worker," *Proceedings*, National Conference for Jewish Social Service, 1933, pp. 7–17; Karpf, M. J.: "Emerging Horizons in Jewish and General Social Work, *ibid*, 1932, pp. 9–15; and *id.*: "Toward a Philosophy for the Jewish Social Worker," *Jewish Social Service Quarterly*, Vol. XI, No. 2, Dec. 1934, pp. 193–196.

[108] "The Relation of the Jewish Social Worker to the Jewish Community. Report of the New York Committee of the Case-Workers Section of the National Conference of Jewish Social Service," *Proceedings*, National Conference of Jewish Social Service, 1934, pp. 82–86; "The Jew and Social and Economic Conditions in the United States" (A paper by a Committee of the Association of Practitioners in Jewish Social Agencies) *Jewish Social Service Quarterly*, Vol. XII, No. 3, March 1936, pp. 298–307; "Labor Approaches to the Jewish Problem," (Paper prepared by a Committee of the Association of Practitioners in Jewish Social Agencies) *Proceedings*, National Conference of Jewish Social Service, 1936, pp. 231–237.

[109] "The History and Activities of the Association of Federation Workers in New York. A Statement Prepared by the Executive Committee of the Association of Federation Social Workers of New York City," *Jewish Social Service Quarterly*, Vol. VIII, No. 4, June 1932, pp. 183–186; Fisher, Jacob: *The Rank and File Movement in Social Work 1931–1936*, New York, The New York School of Social Work, 1936.

[110] Siegel, Mary: "The Practitioner Looks at Jewish Social Work," *Proceedings*, National Conference of Jewish Social Welfare, 1936, pp. 20–22.

[111] Taylor, Maurice: "Employer-Employee Relations in Jewish Social Work," *Proceedings*, National Conference of Jewish Social Service, 1936, pp. 183–191.

[112] See Addendum to paper on "The Jew and Social and Economic Conditions in the United States," presented by Practitioners Group at National Conference of Jewish Social Service, May 1935, *Jewish Social Service Quarterly*, Vol. XII, No. 3, March 1936, pp. 305–307. Also, *The Jewish Social Worker and Labor Zionism, a Statement by the Social Workers' Chapter of the League for Labor Palestine*, New York, 1936, (mimeographed).

The "Reconstructionist philosophy of Jewish Life" refers to the philosophy formulated by Dr. Mordecai M. Kaplan in his *Judaism as a Civilization*, and promulgated by *The Reconstructionist*, a weekly journal published by the group adhering to his point of view.

[113] Taussig, Francis, "The Status of the Jewish Family Welfare Agency," *Proceedings of the 1937 General Assembly*, Council of Jewish Federations and Welfare Funds, Inc., New York, pp. 32–34.

[114] For suggestive summaries see the following: on federation programs, Harry Greenstein, *Proceedings of the 1937 General Assembly*, The Council of Jewish Federation

and Welfare Funds, New York, 1937, pp. 16–19; on child care, Mary Boretz, *ibid,,* pp. 34–36; on Jewish education, William Lewis, *ibid.,* pp. 36–38; on vocational services, Irvin Rosen, *ibid.,* pp. 38–39.

[115] See Younker, Ira M.: "Planning for Community Welfare," *Proceedings of the National Council of Jewish Federations and Welfare Funds,* Chicago, 1934, pp. 18–19. See also Younker, Ira M.: "Does the Federation Structure Fit?" *Proceedings of the 1936 General Assembly,* The National Council of Jewish Federations and Welfare Funds, pp. 14–16; and Hollander, Sidney: "The Changing Scene," *ibid,* pp. 10–13.

[116] *The Federation as the Vital Community Agency. A Report of the Committee on Finances and Governmental Welfare Policies of the National Council of Jewish Federations and Welfare Funds, Frank L. Sulzberger . . . and Ben M. Selekman . . . Co-Chairmen,* New York, National Council of Federations, (1934).

XII

[117] The need for research in social work has been treated in a number of papers and discussions. The following are among the most pertinent: "Research and Leadership" by Ben M. Selekman, *The Menorah Journal,* Vol. XII, No. 2, April-May 1926, pp. 113–126. "Research About Jews" by Leo Wolman, *Proceedings,* National Conference of Jewish Social Service, 1928, pp. 109–113, and Discussions by Goldsmith, S. A., Rubinow, I. M., Hexter, M. B., Slawson, John, *ibid.,* pp. 119–24; 128–35. "Watchmen, What of the Day" by Henry Hurwitz, *The Menorah Journal,* Vol. XII, No. 1, February 1926, pp. 1–21. "Research as an End in Promoting Scientific Social Work," by Raymond Clapp, *Proceedings,* National Conference of Social Work, 1928, pp. 556–560. "Fact Finding and Research as a Basis of Program Making in Social Work" by Neva R. Deardorff, *ibid.,* pp. 415–424.

[118] A thought-provoking presentation of the situation as viewed by a student of Jewish Social Work, is contained in "Jewish Social Work as It Appears to a Student" by Charles Schottland, *Proceedings,* National Conference of Jewish Social Service, 1929, pp. 189–198.

[119] A stimulating presentation of some of these problems by Elisha M. Friedman in the *Union Tidings* of September 1927, prompted the late Julius Rosenwald to offer a number of prizes amounting to $15,000 for the best essays dealing with Judaism in America.

[120] Cf. Karpf, Maurice J.: *The Scientific Basis of Social Work, op. cit.,* references in Index to "Attitudes" and "Norms," pp. 413 and 419 respectively.

[121] For a vigorous discussion of some of these problems see Kallen, Horace M.: "Can Judaism Survive in the United States?" *The Menorah Journal,* Vol. XI, No. 2, April 1925, pp. 101–113.

[122] For a discussion of the relation between the social scientist, social technologist, and social practitioner, see "The Relation Between Schools of Social Work and Social Agencies," by M. J. Karpf, *Proceedings*, National Conference of Social Work, 1925, pp. 651–652.

[123] Cf. Karpf, Maurice J.: "Emerging Horizons in Jewish and General Social Work," *Proceedings*, National Conference of Jewish Social Service, 1932, pp. 13–14.

[124] Sidney and Beatrice Webb, perhaps the foremost students of social amelioration and reform, sum up the situation in *The Prevention of Destitution* as follows:

" . . . . in practically all departments of the work of prevention — in the campaign against infantile mortality, child neglect and preventable disease; in the campaign against mental degeneration and in favor of promotion of better breeding; in the campaign against the ruin of adolescence, the creation of unemployment and the degeneration of the employed, we are always being stopped by the need for further experimenting and additional research. We know enough now to know how supremely important it is to extend our knowledge. But research and experiment in social subjects costs as much as research in chemistry or electricity; and the public does not yet realize this fact! Here, indeed, is a magnificent field for the volunteer worker and for the munificence of many a millionaire. Whether in practical experiment or in pure research there is no range of work that is more likely to bring about immediate social betterment than this of the various means of preventing destitution, and of scientifically treating the cases that occur."

BIBLIOGRAPHY OF REFERENCES

Abrahams, Israel: *Jewish Life in the Middle Ages*, London, Edward Goldston, 1932.

Adler, Evelyn: *The Union Backgrounds, Relationships, and Activities of Selected Members of the International Ladies' Garment Workers' Union, New York, 1933*, Master's Thesis, The Graduate School for Jewish Social Work, 1937.

American Jewish Committee: *The American Jewish Year Book*, Vol. 30, 5689; 31, 5690; 37, 5696; 38, 5697.

———— *Twelfth Annual Report*, New York, 1919.

American Jewish Congress, The: *The Congress Bulletin*, 1936–1937.

———— *What It Is and What It Does*, New York, 1936.

American Jewish Joint Distribution Committee: *Aid to Jews Overseas. Report on the Activities of the American Jewish Joint Distribution Committee for the Year 1935 Including a Brief Resumé for the Year 1936*, New York, 1936.

———— *[Mimeographed Report]*, December 1936.

Asmonean, The, New York, 1849–1858.

Association of Federation Social Workers of New York City: "The History and Activities of the Association of Federation Workers in New York. A Statement Prepared by the Executive Committee of the Association of Federation Social Workers of New York City," *Jewish Social Service Quarterly*, Vol. VIII, No. 4, June 1932, pp. 183–186.

Association of Practitioners in Jewish Social Agencies: "The Jew and Social and Economic Conditions in the United States," (A paper by a Committee of the Association of Practitioners in Jewish Social Agencies), *Jewish Social Service Quarterly*, Vol. XII, No. 3, March 1936, pp. 298–307.

———— "Labor Approaches to the Jewish Problem," (Paper prepared by a Committee of the Association of Practitioners in Jewish Social Agencies), *Proceedings*, National Conference of Jewish Social Service, 1936, pp. 231–237.

Baker, Newton Diehl, Hayes, Carleton J. H. and Straus, Roger Williams: *The American Way, A Study of Human Relations among Protestants, Catholics and Jews*, Chicago, Willett, Clark & Company, 1936.

Bank, Jules: *A Study of 108 Boys Discharged from the Brooklyn Hebrew Orphan Asylum, 1924–1929*, Master's Thesis, The Graduate School for Jewish Social Work, 1936.

Baron, Salo W.: "An Historical Critique of the Jewish Community," *Proceedings*, National Conference of Jewish Social Service, 1935, pp. 44–49.

Barron, Harry I.: *A Study of Leisure Time Interests, Preferences and Activities of Children of the Lower East Side of New York City*, Master's Thesis, The Graduate School for Jewish Social Work, 1935.

Beck, Joseph E.: "Economic Problems Presented to Relief Clients," *Proceedings*, National Conference of Jewish Social Service, 1935, pp. 7–14.

Benderly, Samson: "Jewish Education in the United States," *Proceedings of the 1935 Conference on Jewish Welfare*, National Council of Jewish Federations and Welfare Funds, New York, 1935, pp. 40–42.

Berkson, I.: *Theories of Americanization With Special Reference to the Jewish Group*, New York, Teachers College, Columbia University, 1920.

Bernstein, Ludwig: "Intermarriage and Jewish Social Service," *Jewish Social Service Quarterly*, Vol. V, No. 4, June 1929, pp. 237–241.

———— (Co-author): "Jewish Communal Organization in America," *Proceedings*, National Conference of Jewish Social Service, 1923, pp. 188–199.

B'nai B'rith: *Proceedings of the Fourteenth General Convention of the Constitution Grand Lodge (Changed to Supreme Lodge) B'nai B'rith Held in Washington, D. C. May 4 to 8, 1935*.

Bogen, Boris D.: *Jewish Philanthropy*, New York, Macmillan, 1917.

Bolduan, C. and Weiner, L.: "Causes of Death Among Jews in New York City," *New England Journal of Medicine*, Vol. 208, No. 8, Feb. 23, 1933, pp. 407–416.

Borochov, Ber: *Nationalism and the Class Struggle. A Marxian Approach to the Jewish Problem, Selected Writings*, Introduction by Abraham G. Duker, New York, Poale Zion-Zeire Zion of America and Young Poale Zion Alliance of America, 1937.

Boxerman, William I., *see* Peiser, Kurt and Boxerman, William I.

Breuer, Isaac: *The Jewish National Home*, Translated by Miriam Aumann, Frankfurt a.M., J. Kauffman, 1926.

Britt, George, *see* Broun, Heywood and Britt, George.

Brodie, Israel B.: "Problems and Programs in Palestine," *Proceedings*, National Conference of Jewish Social Service, 1935, pp. 39–43.

Broun, Heywood and Britt, George: *Christians Only*, New York, The Vanguard Press, 1931.

Bruno, Frank J.: "A Romance of Family Case Work, a Review of A Social Audit" by Maurice J. Karpf, *The Survey*, Vol. LV, No. 2, October 15, 1925, pp. 87–89.

Burgess, Ernest W., *see* Park, Robert E. and Burgess, Ernest W.

Burstein, Shulamith: *The Status of National Jewish Youth Organizations in the United States—1933–1934*, Master's Thesis, The Graduate School for Jewish Social Work, 1937.

Case Workers' Section, National Conference of Jewish Social Service, *see* National Conference of Jewish Social Welfare, Case Workers' Section.

Central Conference of American Rabbis, *Proceedings, varia.*

Chalmers, M. M.: *Youth-Serving Organizations*, The American Council on Education, Washington, D. C., 1937.

Chipkin, Israel: "Twenty-Five Years of Jewish Education in the United States," *American Jewish Year Book*, Vol. 38, 5697, 1936–1937, pp. 27–116. Also issued separately by the Jewish Education Association of New York City, 1937.

Clapp, Raymond: "Research as an End in Promoting Scientific Social Work," *Proceedings*, National Conference of Social Work, 1928, pp. 556–560.

Clarke, John H.: *Social Administration Including The Poor Laws*, London, Isaac Pitman and Sons, 1922.

Clinchy, Everett R.: *All in the Name of God*, New York, John Day Company, 1934.

Cohen, Abraham: *Views Regarding Jewish Content in Various Types of Jewish Centers in Relation to Their Aims*, Thesis, The Graduate School for Jewish Social Work, 1936.

Cohen, Armond E.: "A Year in an Organized Jewish Community," *The Reconstructionist*, Vol. 2, No. 19, January 22, 1937, pp. 12–15.

Cohen, J. X.: *Jews, Jobs and Discrimination, A Report on Jewish Non-Employment*, American Jewish Congress, New York, 1937.

Cohen, Morris R.: *Annual Report for 1935, The Work of the Conference on Jewish Relations*, New York, 1937.

——— "As a Liberal Views It," *Proposed Roads for American Jewry, A Symposium*, New York, National Council of Jewish Women. 1936, pp. 51–79.

——— "Jews in Commerce and the Professions," *Proceedings*, National Conference of Jewish Social Service, 1934, pp. 21–28.

———— "A Plea for Liberalism," *Proceedings of the 1935 National Conference on Jewish Welfare*, The National Council of Jewish Federations and Welfare Funds, New York, 1935, pp. 56–58.

Congress Bulletin, The, 1936–1937.

Council of Jewish Federations and Welfare Funds, Inc.

   Federation Financing of Jewish Social Work in 1934, New York, 1935.

   The Federation as the Vital Community Agency. A Report of the Committee on Finances and Governmental Welfare Policies of the National Council of Jewish Federations and Welfare Funds, Frank L. Sulzberger . . . and Ben M. Selekman . . . Co-Chairmen, New York, 1934.

   Proceedings, General Assembly, Chicago, Ill., January 6–7, 1934, New York, 1934.

   Proceedings of the 1935 National Conference on Jewish Welfare, New York, N. Y., January 3 to 6, 1935, New York, 1935.

   Proceedings of the 1936 General Assembly, St. Louis, Mo., January 25–26–27, New York, 1936.

   Proceedings of the 1937 General Assembly, Philadelphia, Pa., January 30–31, 1937, New York, 1937.

   [Year Book] Jewish Social Work, 1934, New York, 1935.

   1935 Year Book of Jewish Social Work (in two parts), New York, 1936.

Cronbach, Abraham: "The Me'il Zedakah," *Hebrew Union College Annual*, Vol. XI, 1936, pp. 503–567.

———— "What Makes Jewish Social Work Jewish? Historical Aspects," *Jewish Social Service Quarterly*, Vol. VII, No. 1, September 1930, pp. 3–5.

Davidson, Gabriel: "The Jew in Agriculture in the United States," *American Jewish Year Book*, Vol. 37, 5696, 1935–1936, pp. 99–134.

Davie, Maurice R.: *World Immigration With Special Reference to the United States*, New York, Macmillan, 1936.

Deardorff, Neva R.: "Fact Finding and Research as a Basis of Program Making in Social Work," *Proceedings*, National Conference of Social Work, 1928, pp. 415–424.

Dinin, Samuel: *Judaism in a Changing Civilization*, New York, Teachers College, Columbia University, 1933.

Drachsler, Julius: *Democracy and Assimilation. The Blending of Immigrant Heritages in America*, New York, Macmillan, 1930.

Dubinsky, G.: "Obstacles in the Development of Foster Family Care for Dependent Children," *Proceedings*, National Conference of Jewish Social Service, 1923, pp. 370–380.

Duker, Abraham G.: "Bibliographical Notes III," *Jewish Social Service Quarterly*, June 1937, Vol. XIII, No. 4, pp. 437–442.

———— "The Problem of Yiddishism," *The Reconstructionist*, Vol. II, No. 20, February 5, 1937, pp. 7–10.

———— "The Theories of Ber Borochov and Their Place in the History of the Jewish Labor Movement" in Ber Borochov: *Nationalism and the Class Struggle. A Marxian Approach to the Jewish Problem. Selected Writings*, New York, Poale Zion-Zeire Zion of America and Young Poale Zion Alliance of America, 1937.

Dushkin, Alexander M.: "Essentials of a Community Program for Jewish Children," *Proceedings*, National Conference of Jewish Social Service, 1934, pp. 114–118.

———— and Honor, Leo L.: "Aims and Activities of Jewish Educational Organizations in America," *Jewish Education*, Vol. V, No. 3, Oct.–Dec. 1933, pp. 136–146.

Eisenstein, Ira: *Creative Judaism*, New York, Behrman's, 1936.

Engelman, Uriah Z.: *The Jewish Community in Figures, Guess-Work and Speculation That Pass for Statistics*, New York, The Jewish Information Bureau, 1937.

———— "The Need for Jewish Population Statistics," *The Menorah Journal*, Vol. XIII, No. 5, November 1927, pp. 467–478.

Feldman, Herman: *Racial Factors in American Industry*, New York, Harper & Bros., 1931.

Ferguson, Charles W.: *Fifty Million Brothers, A Panorama of American Lodges and Clubs*, New York, Farrar and Rinehart, 1937.

Fisher, Galen M., *see* Silcox, Claris Edwin and Fisher, Galen M.

Fisher, Jacob: *The Rank and File Movement in Social Work 1931–1936*, New York, The New York School of Social Work, 1936.

Fleischman, Abraham: *A Study of the Jewish Community of Staten Island, New York, 1936–1937*, Thesis, The Graduate School for Jewish Social Work, 1937.

Frank, H.: "Yiddish in America," *The Zukunft*, Vol. XLII, No. 2, February, 1937, pp. 75–80.

Franklin, Sylvia: *An Analysis of the Case Histories of 92 Children of the New York Hebrew Orphan Asylum*, Thesis, The Graduate School for Jewish Social Work, 1935.

Freund, Michael: "The Community Chest and Its Influence on the Jewish Community," *Jewish Social Service Quarterly*, Vol. VII, No. 2, December 1930, pp. 30–37; *ibid.*, No. 4, June 1931, pp. 27–32.

Frisch, Ephraim: *An Historical Survey of Jewish Philanthropy . . .*, New York, Macmillan, 1924.

Gamoran, Emanuel: *Changing Conceptions in Jewish Education*, New York, Macmillan, 1925.

Gebiner, B.: "The Jewish Labor Committee, Its Establishment and Work," (in Yiddish), *2nd Annual Convention of the Jewish Labor Committee, October 27th, 1935*, New York, 1935.

Gessner, Robert: *Some of My Best Friends Are Jews*, New York, Farrar & Rinehart, 1936.

Glucksman, Harry L.: "Tendencies in the Jewish Center Movement," *Proceedings*, National Conference of Jewish Social Service, 1923, pp. 144–153.

——— Jewish Welfare Board. *Activities. 1935 Report of the Executive Director . . .* , New York, 1936.

——— (Co-author): "Jewish Communal Organization in America," *Proceedings*, National Conference of Jewish Social Service, 1923, pp. 188–199.

Glück, Elsie: "Jewish Workers in the Trade Unions," *Jewish Frontier*, Vol. II, No. 14, December 1935, pp. 11–15.

Goldhamer, Samuel (Co-author): "Jewish Communal Organization in America," *Proceedings*, National Conference of Jewish Social Service, 1923, pp. 188–199.

Goldman, Benjamin B.: *Economic Adjustment of Selected Graduates of the Cleveland Jewish Orphan Home*, Master's Thesis, The Graduate School for Jewish Social Work, 1934.

Goldsmith, Samuel A.: "Factual Materials in Child Care Surveys of the Bureau of Jewish Social Research," *Proceedings*, National Conference of Jewish Social Service, 1927, pp. 228–240.

——— "The Relationship of Jewish Social Work to Public Welfare and Security," *Proceedings of the 1935 National Conference on Jewish Welfare*, National Council of Jewish Federations and Welfare Funds, New York, 1935, pp. 19–22.

——— (Co-author): "Jewish Communal Organization in America," *Proceedings*, National Conference of Jewish Social Service, 1923, pp. 188–199.

Golub, J. J.: "Diseases Among Jews," *Jewish Social Service Quarterly*, Vol. IV, No. 2, Dec. 1927, pp. 144–155.

Graduate School for Jewish Social Work, The: Theses referred to:

Adler, Evelyn: *The Union Backgrounds, Relationships, and Activities of Selected Members of the International Ladies' Garment Workers' Union, New York, 1933.*

Bank, Jules: *A Study of 108 Boys Discharged from the Brooklyn Hebrew Orphan Asylum, 1924–1929.*

Barron, Harry I.: *A Study of Leisure Time Interests, Preferences and Activities of Children of the Lower East Side of New York City.*

Burstein, Shulamith: *The Status of National Jewish Youth Organizations in the United States—1933–1934.*

Cohen, Abraham: *Views Regarding Jewish Content in Various Types of Jewish Centers in Relation to Their Aims.*

Fleischman, Abraham: *A Study of the Jewish Community of Staten Island, New York, 1936–1937.*

Franklin, Sylvia: *An Analysis of the Case Histories of 92 Children of the New York Hebrew Orphan Asylum.*

Goldman, Benjamin B.: *Economic Adjustment of Selected Graduates of the Cleveland Jewish Orphan Home.*

Harris, Dorothy: *Post Institutional Adjustment of 110 Children Discharged from a Child Care Institution.*

Jacobs, Herman: *Some Aspects of the History of the Federation of Jewish Charities Movement.*

Kinzler, Esther: *Some Aspects of the Occupational Distribution of Jews in New York City as Revealed Through a Study of Selected Groups of Names in the New York City Directory for 1933.*

Kohanski, Alexander S.: *The Yiddish Theater in New York, Season of 1932–1933.*

Krems, Julius: *An Analysis of the Case Histories of Children Discharged from Foster Home Care Supervision of the Home Bureau of the H.S.G.S., New York, 1935.*

Langer, Marion: *A Study of the Jewish Community of Easton.*

Margolis, Rose: *History of the Industrial Removal Office.*

Meyer, Lena: *A Study of the Jewish Community of New London, Connecticut, 1936–1937.*

Rabin, Florence: *A Study of Programs in Adult Jewish Educational Organizations in New York City, 1936–37.*

Ramelson, Sylvia L.: *A Study of the Help-Wanted Advertisements in New York Newspapers, 1928, 1931, 1935.*

Rose, Joseph: *Changing Objectives and Practices in Jewish Family Welfare Work, New York City from 1850–1934.*

Shapiro, Tess: *A Study of Jewish Content in a Selected Number of Case Records of a Jewish Family Agency.*

Silver, Harold: *Attitudes of the East European Jewish Immigrants Toward Organized Jewish Charity in the United States, in the Years 1890–1900.*

Unger, Frieda: *Aims and Methods in the Care of Jewish Dependent Children in the United States.*

Wolfe, George, M.D.; *A Study in Immigrant Attitudes and Problems*, 1927–28.

Complete bibliographic references to these works will be found under the proper entries in this bibliography.

Greenstein, Harry: "The Institute on the Social Work Program of Federation," *Proceedings of the 1937 General Assembly*, Council of Jewish Federations and Welfare Funds, New York, 1937, pp. 16–19.

Hadassah News Letter, New York, 1936.

Hadassah, the Women's Zionist Organization of America: *Report National Board, Standing Committees and Regional Unit to the 22nd Annual Convention of Hadassah, Philadelphia, October 18–21, 1936*, [New York, 1936].

Harris, Dorothy: *Post Institutional Adjustment of 110 Children Discharged from a Child Care Institution, New York, 1934–1935*, Thesis, The Graduate School for Jewish Social Work, 1936.

Harrison, Frances N.: "A Health Program for a Jewish Community," *Proceedings*, National Conference of Jewish Social Service, 1924, pp. 164–167.

Hayes, Carleton J. H. *see* Baker, Newton Diehl; Hayes, Carleton J. H. and Straus, Roger Williams.

Hexter, Maurice B.: "Evolutionary Tendencies in the Jewish Federation Movement," *Proceedings*, National Conference of Jewish Social Service, 1926, pp. 9–29.

———— (Co-author): "Jewish Communal Organization in America," *Ibid.*, 1923, pp. 188–199.

HIAS-JCA Emigration-Association (HICEM): *Bulletin d'Information*, 1937.

Hollander, Sidney: "The Changing Scene," *Proceedings of the 1936 General Assembly*, The National Council of Jewish Federations and Welfare Funds, New York, 1936, pp. 10–13.

Honor, Leo L., *see* Dushkin, A. M. and Honor Leo L.

Hoppock, Robert: "General Community Programs for Adjustment," *Proceedings*, National Conference of Jewish Social Service, 1935, pp. 26–28.

Hurwitz, Henry: "Watchmen, What of the Day," *The Menorah Journal*, Vol. XII, No. 1, February 1926, pp. 1–21.

Hurwitz, Maximilian: *The Workmen's Circle. Its History, Ideals, Organization and Institutions*, Workmen's Circle, New York, 1936.

Jacobs, Herman: *Some Aspects of the History of the Federation of Jewish Charities Movement*, Master's Thesis, The Graduate School for Jewish Social Work, 1933.

Janowsky, Oscar I.: *The Jews and Minority Rights*, New York, Columbia University Press, 1933.

Jewish Agricultural Society, The, Inc.: *Annual Report, 1936*.

Jewish Frontier, The, a periodical, New York, 1934–1937.

Jewish Library, The, edited by Leo Jung, New York, Bloch, 1928, 1930, 1934.

Jewish Messenger, The, New York, 1857–1902.

Jewish National Fund: *President's Report Delivered by Dr. Israel Goldstein before the Annual Assembly of the Jewish National Fund, March 1, 1936*, [New York, 1936].

Jewish Reconstructionist Papers, The, edited by Mordecai M. Kaplan, New York, Behrman's, 1936.

Jewish Social Service Association, The: *Fifty Years of Social Service. The History of the United Hebrew Charities of the City of New York. Now The Jewish Social Service Association, Inc.*, published by the Jewish Social Service Association, New York, 1926.

Jewish Social Service Quarterly, The, 1924–1937.

Jewish Times, The, New York, 1869.

Jewish Welfare Board: *Activities, 1935, Report of the Executive Director, Harry L. Glucksman*, New York, 1936.

Jews in America, by the Editors of Fortune, New York, Random House, 1936. Reprinted from *Fortune*, Vol. 13, No. 2, Feb. 1936.

Joseph, Samuel: *Jewish Immigration to the United States from 1881 to 1910*, New York, Columbia University Press, 1914.

Jung, Leo [Editor]: *The Jewish Library*, New York, Bloch, 1928, 1930, 1934.

Kahn, Dorothy, (Co-author): "Jewish Communal Organization in America," *Proceedings*, National Conference of Jewish Social Service, 1923, pp. 188–199.

Kahn, Edward M.: "Present Trends and Tendencies in the Federation Movement," *Proceedings of the 1935 National Conference on Jewish Welfare*, National Council of Jewish Federations and Welfare Funds, New York, 1935, pp. 34–35.

Kallen, Horace M.: "Can Judaism Survive in the United States?," *The Menorah Journal*, Vol. XI, No. 2, April, 1925, pp. 101–113.

———— *Judaism at Bay. Essays Toward the Adjustment of Judaism to Modernity*, New York, Bloch, 1932.

Kaplan, Hyman (Co-author): "Jewish Communal Organizati onin America," *Proceedings*, National Conference of Jewish Social Service, 1923, pp. 188–199.

Kaplan, Mordecai M.: "Is Jewish Unity Possible?" *The Menorah Journal*, Vol. XXV, No. 1, Jan.–March, 1937, pp. 128–131.

———— "Jewish Philanthropy," in *Intelligent Philanthropy*, edited by Ellsworth Faris and Others, Chicago, University of Chicago Press, 1930.

———— *Judaism as a Civilization*, Macmillan, New York, 1934.

———— "The Organization of American Jewry," *Proceedings*, National Conference of Jewish Social Service, 1935, pp. 50–73.

———— [Editor]: *The Jewish Reconstructionist Papers*, New York, Behrman's, 1936.

———— *Judaism in Transition*, New York, Covici Friede, 1936.

Karpf, Fay Berger: *American Social Psychology, Its Origin, Development and European Background*, New York, McGraw-Hill, 1932.

Karpf, Maurice J.: "A Decade of Jewish Philanthropy," *B'nai B'rith Magazine*, Vol. 46, No. 5, February 1932, pp. 145–147, 158.

———— "Discussion of Racial Factors Conditioning Case Work with Jewish Families," *Proceedings*, National Conference of Jewish Social Service, 1924, pp. 33–36.

———— "Emerging Horizons in Jewish and General Social Work," *Ibid.*, 1932, pp. 9–15.

———— "Die Fürsorge für den Einzelfall in Amerika," *Jüdische Wohlfahrtspflege und Sozialpolitik*, Berlin, Sept.–Oct., 1935, Vol. 5 (N. S.) No. 5, pp. 148–156.

———— "Hoichsul far Idishe Sotsiale Arbet in di Fareinigte Shtatn" (A Graduate School for Jewish Social Work in the United States), *Jiwo Bleter*, Vol. V., No. 2, Feb. 1913, pp. 97–108.

———— "National Service Agencies," *Jewish Daily Bulletin*, New York, April 14, 1935, pp. 3, 8; April 17, 1935, p. 2; April 28, 1935, p. 3.

———— "Progress and Problems in Social Work Education During the Depression," Presidential Report to American Association of Schools of Social Work, *Jewish Social Service Quarterly*, Vol. 10, No. 4, June 1934, pp. 257–262.

———— "The Relations of Schools of Social Work to Social Agencies," *Proceedings*, National Conference of Social Work, 1925, pp. 651–652.

———— *The Scientific Basis of Social Work*, New York, Columbia University Press, 1931.

———— *A Social Audit of a Social Service Agency*, Chicago, Jewish Social Service Bureau of Chicago, 1925.

———— *Social Case Work in America*, New York, 1936.

———— "Social Service of National Scope," *Proceedings of the National Conference on Jewish Welfare*, National Council of Jewish Federations and Welfare Funds, New York, 1935, pp. 22–25.

———— "Toward a Philosophy for the Jewish Social Worker," *Jewish Social Service Quarterly*, Vol. XI, No. 2, Dec. 1934, pp. 193–196.

———— "Toward a Source-Book on Jewish Philanthropic Origins" In three parts. Part I, "Biblical Conceptions of Charity," *ibid.*, Vol. XII, No. 3, March 1936, pp. 324–336; Part II, "The Talmudic Period," *ibid.*, No. 4, June, 1936, pp. 396–410; Part III," Biblical Excerpts on Benevolence," *ibid.*, Vol. XIII, No. 2, Dec. 1936, pp. 297–303.

———— "To What End Jewish Education," *The American Hebrew*, Vol. CXL, No. 16, March 5, 1937, pp. 948–968.

———— "The Training School for Jewish Social Work, Its Program, Possibilities and Limitations," *Proceedings*, National Conference of Jewish Social Service, 1925, pp. 11–41.

———— "Wanted—A Return to Basic Values," *Jewish Social Service Quarterly*, Vol. VIII, No. 2, Dec. 1931, pp. 58–63.

Kaufman, Fritz: "Public Employment Services and Social Agencies" *Proceedings*, National Conference of Jewish Social Service, 1936, pp. 206–210.

Kerstein, Solomon (editor): *Jubilee Volume of the Michael Tenzer Family Circle. Tenth Anniversary 1927–1937. A Record of the Activities and Achievements of the Michael Tenzer Family Circle* . . . New York, [1937].

Kinzler, Esther: *Some Aspects of the Occupational Distribution of Jews in New York City as Revealed Through a Study of Selected Groups of Names in the New York City Directory for 1933*, Thesis, The Graduate School for Jewish Social Work, New York, 1935.

Kittner, Violet: "What Makes Jewish Social Work 'Jewish'? As the Case Worker Senses It." *Jewish Social Service Quarterly*, Vol. VII, No. 1, September, 1930, pp. 8–10.

Kohanski, Alexander S.: *The Yiddish Theater in New York. Season of 1932–1933*, Thesis, The Graduate School for Jewish Social Work, New York, 1933.

Kohn, Eugene: *The Future of Judaism in America*, New Rochelle, N. Y., The Liberal Press, 1934.

Kohs, S. C.: "Current Fallacies Regarding Jewish Social Work," *Jewish Social Service Quarterly*, Vol. IX, No. 3, June 1933, pp. 296–305.

———— "Economic Problems in Smaller Communities," *Proceedings*, National Conference of Jewish Social Service, 1935, pp. 20–25.

———— "Jewish Content in Jewish Social Work," *ibid.*, 1936, pp. 99–113.

Krems, Julius: *An Analysis of the Case Histories of Children Discharged from Foster Home Care Supervision of the Home Bureau of the H. S. G. S., New York, 1935*, Thesis, The Graduate School for Jewish Social Work, 1937.

Kreutzberger, Max: "Problems and Programs in Central Europe," *Proceedings*, National Conference of Jewish Social Service, 1935, pp. 33–38.

Labor Zionist News Letter, a periodical, New York, 1937.

Langer, Marion: *A Study of the Jewish Community of Easton*, Master's Thesis, The Graduate School for Jewish Social Work, 1936.

Lasker, Bruno (Editor): *Jewish Experiences in America*, New York, The Inquiry, 1930.

———— "Jewish Handicaps in the Employment Market," *Jewish Social Service Quarterly*, Vol. II, No. 3, March 1926, pp. 170–177.

Lazaron, Morris S.: *Judaism's Message to the World*, 1937.

Lazarus, Isidore: "In Defense of the 'Accidental' Jew," *The Menorah Journal*, Vol. XVI, No. 4, April 1929, pp. 335–345.

League for Labor Palestine. Social Workers' Chapter: *The Jewish Social Worker and Labor Zionism, a Statement by the Social Workers' Chapter of the League for Labor Palestine*, New York, 1936.

Leavitt, Moses A.: "The Self-Support Department of the J.S.S.A." in *Handicapped Wage Earners*, New York, Jewish Social Service Association, 1928.

Lehrer, Leibush: "The Jewish Secular School," *Jewish Education*, Vol. 8, No. 1, Jan.–Mar. 1936, pp. 33–42. Also *Jewish Social Service Quarterly*, Vol. XII, No. 3, March 1936, pp. 308–317.

Lestchinsky, Jacob: "The Number of Jews in the World," *Jiwo Bleter*, Vol. IX, No. 4–5, April–May, 1936, pp. 161–198.

Levinger, Lee J.: *The Jewish Student in America*, The B'nai B'rith Hillel Foundation, Cincinnati, Ohio, 1937.

———— "Surveying the Jewish Students," *B'nai B'rith Magazine*, Vol. 51, No. 7, pp. 214, 234–35.

Levitsky, Louis M.: "The Story of an Awakened Community," *The Reconstructionist*, Vol. 1, No. 20, February 7, 1936, pp. 7–14.

Lewisohn, Ludwig (Ed.): *Rebirth. A Book of Modern Jewish Thought*, New York, Harper, 1935.

Linfield, H. S.: "The Communal Organization of the Jews in the United States, 1927," *American Jewish Year Book*, Vol. 31, 5690, pp. 99–254.

———— "Jewish Congregations in the United States," *ibid.*, Vol. 30, 5689, pp. 199–200.

———— "The Jewish Population in the United States 1927," *ibid.*, pp. 101–108.

Lowenstein, Solomon: "Jewish Needs and Welfare Facilities Today," *Proceedings of the 1935 National Conference on Jewish Welfare*, National Council of Jewish Federations and Welfare Funds, New York, 1935, pp. 13–17.

———— (Co-author): "Jewish Communal Organization in America," *Proceedings*, National Conference of Jewish Social Service, 1923, pp. 188–189.

Lurie, Harry: "Essentials of a Community Program for Jewish Children," *Proceedings*, National Conference of Jewish Social Service, 1934, pp. 109–114.

———— "Is Jewish Unity Possible?" *The Menorah Journal*, Vol. XXIV, No. 3, Oct.–Dec., 1936, pp. 219–227; "A Rejoinder," *ibid.*, Vol. XXV, No. 1, Jan.–March, 1937, pp. 131–133.

———— "Some Problems in the Collection and Interpretation of Jewish Population Data," *Jewish Social Service Quarterly*, Vol. X, No. 4, June 1934, pp. 263–268.

———— "Suggestions for Jewish Occupational Programs," *Proceedings*, National Conference of Jewish Social Service, 1936, pp. 217–221.

———— "What Makes Jewish Social Work 'Jewish'? The Evidence from a Social Agency." *Jewish Social Service Quarterly*, Vol. VII, No. 1, September 1930, pp. 5–8.

Lvovitch, David: "Problems and Programs in Eastern Europe," *Proceedings*, National Conference of Jewish Social Service, 1935, pp. 30–32.

McGill, Nettie Pauline: "The Religio-Cultural Backgrounds of New York City's Youth," *Better Times*, Vol. XVIII, No. 27, April 1937, pp. 22–28.

Maller, J. B.: "The Maladjusted Jewish Child," *Jewish Social Service Quarterly*, Vol. IX, No. 3, June 1933, pp. 285–295, and Vol. X, No. 2, Dec. 1933, pp. 157–162.

Malzberg, Benjamin: "New Data Relative to Incidence of Mental Disease Among Jews," *Mental Hygiene*, April 1936, pp. 280–291.

Margolis, Rose: *History of the Industrial Removal Office*, Thesis, The Graduate School for Jewish Social Work, New York, 1935.

Meyer, Lena: *A Study of the Jewish Community of New London, Conn., 1936–1937*, Thesis, The Graduate School for Jewish Social Work.

Miller, Herbert A.: *Races, Nations, and Classes*, Philadelphia, Lippincott, 1924.

———— *see also* Park, Robert E. and Miller, Herbert E.

Mizrachi Jubilee Publication of the Mizrachi Organization of America (1911–1936), Edited by P. Churgin and Leon Gellman, New York, 1936.

Moss, M. *see* Slawson, J. and Moss M.

Mount Sinai Hospital of the City of New York: *83rd Annual Report, 1935*.

National Conference of Jewish Charities, *see*, National Conference of Jewish Social Welfare

National Conference of Jewish Social Service, *see* National Conference of Jewish Social Welfare.

National Conference of Jewish Social Welfare (formerly National Conference of Jewish Social Service, and National Conference of Jewish Charities). *The Jewish Social Service Quarterly*, 1924–1937, *Proceedings*, 1900, 1902, 1904, 1906, 1908, 1910, 1912, 1918, 1923–1936.

National Conference of Jewish Social Welfare, Case-Workers' Section: "The Relation of the Jewish Social Worker to the Jewish Community. Report of the New York Committee of the Case-Workers' Section of the National Conference of Jewish Social Service," *Proceedings*, National Conference of Jewish Social Service, 1934, pp. 82–86.

National Council of Jewish Federations and Welfare Funds *see* Council of Jewish Federations and Welfare Funds, Inc.

Neuburger, Otto: "Jewish Experience with Government Occupational Adjustment Programs in Pre-Hitler Germany," *Proceedings*, National Conference of Jewish Social Service, 1936, pp. 211–216.

New Palestine, The, New York, 1936–1937.

Occident, The, New York, 1843–1850.

ORT Union: *Report of the Executive of the Central Board of the ORT Union Submitted to its Primary Session, Paris, September 7–9, 1936.*

Palevsky, Mary: "Neighborhood Interference and Cooperation in Case Work with Jewish Families," *Proceedings*, National Conference of Jewish Social Service, 1924, pp. 37–48.

Park, Robert E., and Burgess, Ernest W.: *Introduction to the Science of Sociology*, Chicago, University of Chicago Press, 1924.

———— and Miller, Herbert A.: *Old World Traits Transplanted*, Chicago, Society for Social Research, University of Chicago, 1925.

Peiser, Kurt and Boxerman, William I.: *Forward Steps in Jewish Community Organization—Recent Experiences in Detroit*, Jewish Welfare Federation of Detroit, 1936.

Practitioners in Jewish Social Agencies *see* Association of Practitioners in Jewish Social Agencies.

Rabbinical Assembly of the Jewish Theological Seminary of America: *Proceedings, varia.*

Rabin, Florence: *A Study of Programs in Adult Jewish Educational Organizations in New York City, 1936–37*, Thesis, The Graduate School for Jewish Social Work, 1937.

Rabinoff, George W.: "Where Is Jewish Social Work Going?" *Jewish Social Service Quarterly*, Vol. IX, No. 2, March 1933, pp. 252–255.

Ramelson, Sylvia L.: *A Study of the Help-Wanted Advertisements in New York Newspapers, 1928, 1931, 1935*, Thesis, The Graduate School for Jewish Social Work, New York, 1936.

Reconstructionist, The, New York, 1935–1937.

Richmond, Mary: *What Is Social Case Work*, New York, The Russell Sage Foundation, 1922.

Robison, Sophia M.: *Can Delinquency Be Measured*, New York, Columbia University Press, 1936.

Rose, Joseph: *Changing Objectives and Practices in Jewish Family Welfare Work.* Thesis, The Graduate School for Jewish Social Work, 1934.

Rosen, Irvin: "Occupational Adjustment Problems among Jews," *Proceedings*, National Conference of Jewish Social Service, 1935, pp. 15–19.

———— *see* also Steinberg, Janet and Rosen, Irvin.

Rubinow, I. M.: "The Credo of a Jewish Social Worker," *Proceedings*, National Conference of Jewish Social Service, 1933, pp. 7–17.

———— "The Economic and Industrial Status of American Jewry," *ibid.*, 1932, pp. 28–38.

———— "Jews Without Jobs," *Jewish Frontier*, Vol. II, No. 2, December 1934, pp. 17–18; "Economics of Anti-Semitism," *ibid.*, Vol. II, No. 4, February, 1935, pp. 19–22; "Middle-Class into Proletariat," *ibid.*, Vol. II, No. 6, April 1936, pp. 10–14.

———— "Racial Factors Which Condition Case Work with Jewish Families," *Proceedings*, National Conference of Jewish Social Service, 1924, pp. 22–32.

Ryckoff, Irving: *A Study of Organizational Affiliations and Activities of the Jewish Population of Staten Island, New York, 1936–1937*, Thesis, The Graduate School for Jewish Social Work.

Saltzman, R.: *Tsu der Geshichte fun der Fraternaler Bavegung*, New York, International Workers Order, 1936.

Sayles, Mary Buell: *Substitute Parents. A Study of Foster Families*, New York, The Commonwealth Fund, 1936.

Schechter, Solomon: "Notes of Lectures on Jewish Philanthropy," *Studies in Judaism, Third Series*, Philadelphia, Jewish Publication Society, 1924, pp. 238–276. Also prepared for publication by Jacob Bosniak and reprinted separately, Philadelphia, Jewish Publication Society, 1925.

Schneiderman, Harry: "Jewish War Relief Work," *American Jewish Year Book*, 5678, 1917–1918, pp. 194–226.

Schottland, Charles I.: "Jewish Social Work as It Appears to a Student," *Proceedings*, National Conference of Jewish Social Service, 1929, pp. 189–198.

Schulman, Samuel: "Israel," *Yearbook*, Central Conference of American Rabbis, Vol. XLV, 1935, pp. 260–311.

Selekman, Ben: "Jewish Community Programs for Adjustment," *Proceedings*, National Conference of Jewish Social Service, 1935, p. 29.

Seman, Philip L.: "The Jewish Spirit in Community Centers," *Jewish Social Service Quarterly*, Vol. II, June 1926, pp. 258–264.

———— "The Place of Character Development Agencies in Our Jewish Social Service Program," *ibid.*, Vol. VIII, No. 1, Sept. 1931, pp. 9–18.

Shapiro, Tess: *A Study of Jewish Content in a Selected Number of Case Records of a Jewish Family Agency*, Thesis, The Graduate School for Jewish Social Work, 1937.

———— "Planning for Jewish Economic Welfare," *ibid.*, 1934, pp. 28–33.

———— "Research and Leadership," *The Menorah Journal*, Vol. XII, No. 2, April-May 1926, pp. 113–126.

———— (Co-Chairman), *see* Council of Jewish Federations and Welfare Funds: *The Federation as the Vital Community Agency* . . .

Siegel, Mary: "The Practitioner Looks at Jewish Social Work," *Proceedings*, National Conference of Jewish Social Welfare, 1936, pp. 20–22.

Silcox, Claris Edwin and Fisher, Galen M.: *Catholics, Jews and Protestants. A Study of Relationships in the United States and Canada*, New York, Harper, 1934.

Silver, Harold: *Attitudes of the East European Jewish Immigrants Toward Organized Jewish Charity in the United States, in the Years 1890–1900*. Master's Thesis, The Graduate School for Jewish Social Work, New York, 1934.

Simon, Max: "The Conflict Around the Cleveland Community Council," *The Congress Bulletin*, Vol. 3, No. 13, January 1, 1933, pp. 3–4.

Slawson, John: "Care and Treatment of the Problem Child," *Proceedings*, National Conference of Jewish Social Service, 1935, pp. 156–163.

———— "What Makes Jewish Social Work Jewish? Communal Aspects." *Jewish Social Service Quarterly*, Vol. VII, No. 1, September 1930, pp. 11–14.

———— and Moss M.: "Mental Illness Among Jews," *Jewish Social Service Quarterly*, Vol. XIII, No. 4, June 1936, pp. 343–350.

Staff, Clement: *An Introduction to the Yiddishist Movement in the United States*, Thesis, The Graduate School for Jewish Social Work, 1937.

Steinberg, Janet and Rosen, Irvin: "Survey of Jewish Occupational Adjustment Programs," *Proceedings*, National Conference of Jewish Social Service, 1936, pp. 198–205.

Straus, Roger Williams, *see* Baker, Newton Diehl; Hayes, Carleton J. H. and Straus, Roger Williams.

Strauss, Israel: "A Medical School Associated with a Jewish Hospital," *Proceedings*, National Conference of Jewish Social Service, 1932, pp. 179–184.

Sulzberger, Frank L., (Co-Chairman), *see* Council of Jewish Federations and Welfare Funds, Inc.: *The Federation as the Vital Community Agency* . . .

Symposium on "Jewish Economic Adjustment Problems and Programs," *Proceedings*, National Conference of Jewish Social Service, 1935, pp. 7–43.

Symposium on "Jewish Social Research": *Proceedings*, National Conference of Jewish Social Service, 1928, pp. 109–113, 119–124; 128–135.

Symposium on "Jewish Vocational Service Agencies," *Proceedings*, National Conference of Jewish Social Welfare, 1936, pp. 198–221.

Symposium on "What Makes Jewish Social Work 'Jewish'?", *Jewish Social Service Quarterly*, Vol. VII, No. 1, September 1930, pp. 3–14.

Taussig, Frances, "The Status of the Jewish Family Welfare Agency," *Proceedings of the 1937 General Assembly*, Council of Jewish Federations and Welfare Funds, Inc., New York, pp. 32–34.

———— (Co-author): "Jewish Communal Organization in America," *Proceedings*, National Conference of Jewish Social Service, 1923, pp. 188–199.

Taylor, Maurice: "Employer-Employee Relations in Jewish Social Work," *Proceedings*, National Conference of Jewish Social Service, 1936, pp. 183–191.

Thurston, Henry W.: *The Dependent Child*, New York, Columbia University Press, 1930.

Trotskey, Elias L.: *The Education of Dependent Children. A Survey of the Educational Policies, Practices and Problems of the Three Child-Caring Organizations Affiliated with the Jewish Charities of Chicago*, Chicago, 1935 (mimeographed).

———— *Institutional Care and Placing-Out*, Chicago, The Marks Nathan Jewish Orphan Home, 1930.

Unger, Frieda: *Aims and Methods in the Care of Jewish Dependent Children in the United States*. Master's Thesis, The Graduate School for Jewish Social Work, New York, 1935.

Union of American Hebrew Congregations, *The Sixty-Second Annual Report*, 1936.

United Hebrew Charities: *Annual Reports*.

United Synagogue of America: "Report of the National Convention, Washington, D. C., March, 1936," *The United Synagogue News*, Vol. 1, No. 2, April, 1936.

Valentin, Hugo: *Anti-Semitism*, New York, The Viking Press, 1936.

Waldman, Morris D.: "The Galveston Movement," *The Jewish Social Service Quarterly*, Vol. IV, No. 3, March 1928, pp. 197–206.

———— "The International Scene in Jewish Life," *Proceedings*, National Conference of Jewish Social Service, 1932, pp. 19–25.

———— "Jewish Morale in the Present Situation," *Proceedings*, National Conference of Jewish Social Welfare, 1937.

———— "Problems Facing the Jews Throughout the World and Their Implications for American Jewry," *Proceedings*, National Conference of Jewish Social Service, 1934, pp. 54–56.

Webb, Sidney and Beatrice: *The Prevention of Destitution*, New York, Longmans, 1911.

Weiner, L., *see* Bolduan C., and Weiner, L.

Weiss, Hiram B.: "A Suggestion for a Health Program for a Jewish Community," *Proceedings*, National Conference of Jewish Social Service, 1924, pp. 150–164.

Weitz, Sidney: "The Significance of the Cleveland Community Council," *Proceedings of the 1937 General Assembly*, Council of Jewish Federations and Welfare Funds, New York, 1937, pp. 10–11.

Wiesenfeld, Leo: "The Conflict Around the Cleveland Council," *The Congress Bulletin*, Vol. 3, No. 13, January 1, 1936, pp. 3–4.

Willen, Joseph: "Present Trends and Tendencies in the Federation Movement," *Proceedings of the 1935 National Conference on Jewish Welfare*, National Council of Jewish Federations and Welfare Funds, New York, 1935, pp. 26–29.

———— "Where Is The Money Coming From to Meet Increased Local and Overseas Needs?", *Proceedings of the 1936 General Assembly*, National Council of Jewish Federations and Welfare Funds, New York, 1936, pp. 17–21.

Wolman, Leo: "Research about the Jews," *Proceedings*, National Conference of Jewish Social Service, 1928, pp. 109–113.

Young Judaea: *Year Book, 1935–36*, New York, 1936.

Younker, Ira M.: "Does the Federation Structure Fit?" *Proceedings of the 1936 General Assembly*, The National Council of Jewish Federations and Welfare Funds, pp. 14–16.

———— "Planning for Community Welfare," *Proceedings of the National Council of Jewish Federations and Welfare Funds*, Chicago, 1934, pp. 18–19.

Zeitgeist, Der, New York, 1880–1882.

Zionist Organization of America: *Report of the Administrative Committee to the 39th Annual Convention of the Zionist Organization of America held at the Biltmore Hotel, Providence, Rhode Island, July 4 and continuing through July 7, 1936*, New York, 1936.

INDEX

Accounting, Jews in, 16, 18, 19

Addams, Jane, and immigrant adjustment, 38

Adjustment of Jews in U.S.A., programs of, 42–50; and social work, 140–149; summary on, 171–173; and survival problem, 41

Advertising, Jews in, 10, 16

Advertisements and discrimination, 21–22

Age distribution, of Jewish youth, 6–7; of Jews, 5

Aged, Jewish, institutions for, expenditures on, 68; present status of, 96, 148–149; summary on, 176

Agencies, national, classification and description of, 116–129; and depression 139–140; expenditures of, 68; for social work, 118–122; summary on, 178–180

Agriculture, Jews in, 14, 17–18, 124; early experiments of, 78; and ORT, 126

Agro-Joint, activities of, 124

Akron, Ohio, contributors to Jewish federation compared with population of, 105

Amaurotic family idiocy, among Jews, 84

American Academy for Jewish Research, 133

American Association of Schools of Social Work, 120

American Economic Committee for Palestine, 128

American Federation of Labor, and Jewish groups affiliated with, 65, 144–146

American Friends of the Hebrew University, 118, 128, 179

American Jewish Committee, 117, 173; activities, establishment and policies of, 62–65; and census, 1–2

American Jewish Congress, 117, 173; activities, establishment and policies of, 63–65, 191–192 n. 42

American Jewish Historical Society, 133

American Jewish Joint Agricultural Corporation, see Agro-Joint

American Jewish Joint Distribution Committee (J.D.C., Joint), 118; campaigns of, 128–129, 180; contributors to, 106–107; history and activities of, 123–126; summary on, 178–179

American Jewish Physicians Committee, 128, 179

American Joint Reconstruction Foundation, 124

American Palestine Campaign, 118, 127, 179

American Palestine Fund, 129

Americanization, modern concepts of, 38–40; older concepts of, 37–38; see also Immigrants; Immigration.

Amusement field, Jews in, 10, 11

Anti-Defamation League, see B'nai B'rith Anti-Defamation League

Anti-nationalists, attitudes of, 43–45, 47; see also Assimilation, Non-nationalists, Non-Zionists

Anti-Semitism in U.S.A., 22–28; and community chests, 109–110; and employment, 18–22, 160–161; (of Jews, 21); and government, 21, 25; needed research on, 161–162; propaganda of, 23–26; struggle against, 23, 62–66, 117, 173; summary on, 170

Architecture, and Jews, 16

Ardmore, Contributors to Jewish federation, compared with population of, 105

Art, and Jews, 16

Artisans, and ORT, 126

Assimilation, ideology of, 49–50; needed studies of, 157–159; and social work, 140–142, 143–146, 148–149, 190 n. 28 f.; see also Anti-nationalists, Non-nationalists

Austria, Jewish immigrants from, 6

Automobile industry, Jews in, 10, 16

Aviation, Jews in, 16

of overseas relief, 123–126, 128–129; of Palestine activities, 44, 127–129; of religious work, 67; of social work, 68, 100, 139, 140; *see also* Expenditures

Fishing industry, Jews in, 14

Food industry, Jews in, 11

Ford, Henry, and anti-Semitism, 23

Forestry, Jews in, 14

Fortune, study of Jewish participation in American life made and published by, 9–11

Foster homes for Jewish children, 92–95; *see also* Child welfare

Fraternal orders, Jewish, 52, 130, 180, 198, n. 96; *see also* B'nai B'rith

Fraternities, Greek letter, and Jewish, 132

Friedman, Elisha M., 201, n. 119

Friedman, (name), occupational distribution of, 12

Galveston Movement, for immigrant distribution, 5

German Jewish Children's Aid, Inc., 118, 122, 178

German Jews, in U.S.A., early immigration wave, 74; and East European immigrants, 40–41, 74, 76–78; philanthropies of, 75–76; present refugees, 5, 29–30, 32–33, 118, 121–122, 126, 178, 179

Germany, Jews in, activities for, 124–127; assimilated, 50; *see also* Boycott; German Jews; Nazism

Ginsburg (name), occupational distribution of, 12

Goldberg (name), occupational distribution of, 12

Goldstein (name), occupational distribution of, 12

Governors, Jewish, in U.S.A., 24

Graduate School for Jewish Social Work, 117, 119–120, 133, 168, 178

Guilds, medieval, and Jews, 161

Hadassah, The Women's Zionist Organization of America, 44, 118, 127–128, 179

Harvard University, Jewish library in, 133

Health care, Jewish, in Palestine, 127–128; in U.S.A., 68, 84–91, 148–149, 174; *see also* Diseases; Hospitals; Medicine; Physicians

Hebraists, and Jewish adjustment, 47–48

Hebrew High Schools, 59

Hebrew Immigrant Aid Society, (HIAS), 36, 118, 178

Hebrew language, education in, 47–48, 59; as mother tongue, 1; press in, 134

Hebrew Sheltering Guardian Society, and child care, 93

Hebrew Theological College in Chicago, 133

Hebrew Union College, 53, 54, 133, 191 n. 33

Hebrew University in Jerusalem, 44, 118, 123; Hospital and Post-Graduate Medical School of, 128, 179

Heder, (*Hedarim*), 58, 173

Hekdesh, 85

HIAS, *see* Hebrew Immigrant Aid Society

HICEM, 36, 124

High Commission for German Refugees, 124

High Holidays, observance of, 52; and population statistics, 2

Hillel Foundations, 100, 176

Hitler regime, *see* Nazism

Hoover administration, and immigration, 32

Home for Chronic Invalids, *see* Montefiore Hospital

Home, Jewish, decline of, 155

Homeless, Jewish, expenditures on, 68; in Middle Ages, 71

Hospitals, Jewish, 178; for chronic diseases, 88–91; expenditures on, 86–87, 174; history of, 85–86, 89–90; for mental diseases, 87; national, 117–118; need for, 84–85; statistics of, 86–87; summary on, 174

Hospitals, non-Jewish, and Jewish physicians, and interns, 18–19

ICA, *see* Jewish Colonization Association

Illinois, Jewish governor in, 24

Immigrants, Jewish, adjustment of, 36–41, 118, 171; *see also* Americanization